**W9-BWS-952**

Presented to:

_____

Presented by:

_____

Date:

_____

# MORE E-MAIL FROM GOD FOR TEENS

by

Claire Cloninger & Curt Cloninger

Honor Books
Tulsa, Oklahoma

*More E-Mail from God for Teens*
ISBN 1-56292-931-3
Copyright © 2000 by Claire Cloninger & Curt Cloninger
Represented by: Alive Communications, Inc.
7680 Goddard Street
Suite 200
Colorado Springs, CO 80920

Published by Honor Books
P.O. Box 55388
Tulsa, Oklahoma 74155

Printed in the United States of America. All rights reserved under International Copyright Law. Contents and/or cover may not be reproduced in whole or in part in any form without the express written consent of the Publisher.

## CLAIRE'S DEDICATION

For Alan and Kellie and the youth group at Christ Church,
Mobile, Alabama, and for all the youth pastors and
youth groups across this country who are showing
Jesus to the world around them every day.

## CURT'S DEDICATION

For Rophe & Nissi, Matt Harris, Laura, Tiffany, Elizabeth Lovell,
Katie Murphy, Daniel Sanford, Jacob Ingersoll, and all
the other warriors in this next wave of God's army.

## *INTRODUCTION*

What is God like? Is He like the school principal who's constantly frowning and giving lectures? When you dial His number, do you always get a busy signal? Does He hang out a "Gone-to-Lunch" sign and lock up the God-shop whenever people start getting on His nerves? Or maybe He's like a wimpy little clerk in life's candy store, just waiting to give you exactly what you want when you want it.

There are a million wrong ideas circulating about God. But God wants you to have the right idea. He wants you to understand that He's the awesome Creator who made you and loves you. He wants you to know Him as a loving Father who's proud of you, His child. He wants you to discover that He's a best friend who'll stick by you through whatever life throws at you, from now until forever. And you don't have to wander around in outer space trying to get in touch with Him. He's already trying to get in touch with you. That's why He's filling up your in-box with personal e-mails—written to you and signed with love from Him.

So log on right now and begin the adventure of knowing Him personally. It'll change your life forever. That's a promise!!!

# THE BUTTERFLY PRINCIPLE

**Stop judging by mere appearances,
and make a right judgment.**

**John          7:24**

-------------------------------------------

My Child,

>Things aren't always what they seem. A caterpillar looks like it will never be anything but a belly-crawling grub, and then it sprouts wings and flies around in glorious color. In winter, it looks like all the trees are dead. Then spring rolls around, and those same trees are full of blossoms and green leaves. You should know just from looking at nature that there's more to life than meets the eye.

The same is true with people. Don't give up on anybody. The shyest person may turn out to be full of exciting stories and funny jokes. The meanest bully might have a favorite kitten named Fluffy. I created humans in My image, and I'm full of surprises. Expect to find the good in people, and in time, you will see them as I see them—worthy of great love and respect.

Your Creator,
>God

== == ==    == == == == == == == == ==

# TAKE A CHILL PILL

**In your anger do not sin; when you are on
your beds, search your hearts and be silent.**

**Psalm**      **4:4**

-------------------------------------------

My Child,

>Has anyone ever told you, "Just sleep on it"? That's often good advice. Sometimes you'll be so angry about something that you can't see straight. That is not a good time to make a decision. When you're angry, you may blurt out something rude and later think, *I can't believe I said that.*

My advice is, just wait. When you're mad, don't act. If someone is forcing you to make a decision while you're mad, tell them, "I need some time to think about this. Let me get back to you." Then just chill out and pray about it. Ask Me what I think about the situation. Breathe deeply. Count to a hundred. Do whatever it takes to calm down. Yes, you have emotions. But you don't have to be a slave to them. I want you to control your emotions, not the other way around.

Your Peace,
>God

== == ==    == == == == == == == == ==

# ALWAYS HAVE BEEN AND ALWAYS WILL BE

**The LORD, is the Rock eternal.**

Isaiah 26:4

---------------------------------------------

My Child,

>Eternity is a mindblower. One writer described it like this: Imagine every grain of sand in the world in one huge pile. Once every million years, a bird comes and takes a single grain of sand away from the pile. Once that pile of sand is finally gone, the bird has to bring all the sand back in the same way and take it away again a million more times. In all that time, only a fraction of one second of eternity will have passed. I am eternal.

If you put a rough stone into a rushing river, eventually that stone will be polished smooth. If you leave the stone in longer, it will eventually be ground to sand. But I am the Rock eternal. I will never grind down. I am as strong and dependable today as I have ever been. I will always be strong and dependable. So depend on Me. I will never let you down.

Your Rock,
>God

== == ==   == == == == == == == == ==

# WHO'S #1?

**I am the LORD your God, who brought you out of Egypt, out of the land of slavery. You shall have no other gods before me.**

**Deuteronomy        5:6-7**

---------------------------------------------

My Child,

>Would you have more than one boyfriend or girlfriend at the same time? Maybe, but not for long. You would eventually favor one or the other. (Probably both would leave you, disgusted with your indecision.)

There's no tie for the No. 1 team in the NBA finals. It's the same with Me. I will not share the trophy of your love with any other god. Do you like Me 50 percent and music 50 percent? Do you like Me 50 percent and *Star Wars* 50 percent? I don't mind you liking other things, but if you like anything as much as Me, you will eventually begin to like it more than Me. That's just the way it works. There can only be one No. 1. I'm asking you to make Me your No. 1. You are My No. 1. I hope you know that.

The First,
>God

== == ==    == == == == == == == == ==

# SAY WHAT?

**You shall not misuse the name of the Lord your God, for the Lord will not hold anyone guiltless who misuses his name.**

Deuteronomy          5:11

---

Dear Child,

>There are lots of ways to misuse My name besides tacking a cuss word onto the end of it. If you say, "God told me to go to the mall," but I never told you that, you just misused My name. If you say, "God doesn't mind if I smoke," but I never told you that, you just misused My name. If you say, "God doesn't really care whether we believe in Jesus, as long as we believe in something," you just misused My name.

There are lots of people on earth misquoting and misrepresenting Me, teaching people that I'm someone other than who I am. To really know who I am, read the Bible. Every word in that book is 100 percent Me. You wouldn't like someone walking around saying things about you that weren't true. I don't like it either. Before you begin to teach someone who I am, find out who I am for yourself. Read My Bible. Get to know the real Me.

The Truth,
>God

== == ==    == == == == == == == == ==

# MAKE IT RIGHT

**If you are offering your gift at the altar and there remember that your brother has something against you, leave your gift there in front of the altar. First go and be reconciled to your brother; then come and offer your gift.**

Matthew          5:23-24

---------------------------------------------

My Child,

>I want you to keep short accounts. That means I don't want you to be mad at anyone for long. I understand people get on your nerves— brothers, sisters, friends, and enemies. But I want you to be at peace with those around you. If you feed the homeless, you're nice to the kids called nerds, and you wear an "I Love Jesus" shirt, but you hate your big brother because he made fun of you, how are you worshiping Me?

You show your love for Me by loving and forgiving the people around you. If you have to choose between writing Me a love song or apologizing to someone, I want you to apologize first. Then the love song you write will flow from a heart of love. I care about your relationships, and I want them to be right.

Your Friend,
>God

== == ==    == == == == == == == == ==

# LET IT GO

**Love your enemies and pray for
those who persecute you.**

**Matthew          5:44**

------------------------------------------

Dear Child,

>When you cut yourself or get a bruise, your body eventually heals. Your body doesn't say, "I hate you, sticker bush! You've injured me, and I'll never forgive you. I'll carry this cut around with me forever to remind me of how evil you are!" Your body knows that type of unforgiving behavior just hurts itself. Staying cut is not going to affect the sticker bush one way or another.

Likewise, if someone cuts you down with mean words, don't carry those words around. You're only hurting yourself. One of the best ways to heal from an emotional wound is to pray a blessing on the person who hurt you. I know it sounds crazy, but praying for your enemies keeps their mean words from controlling you. I want you to love everybody. I'll help you do it.

Your Healer,
>God

== == ==    == == == == == == == == ==

# WHAT DO YOU THINK "ENOUGH" IS?

**You shall not covet . . . anything
that belongs to your neighbor.**

**Deuteronomy          5:21**

---------------------------------------------

My Child,

>Jealousy is an ugly thing. It's one thing to admire someone's new car.
It's another thing to sit up late every night wishing that car were yours.
When you wish you had someone else's stuff, it can lead to stealing.
But even if it doesn't lead to stealing, it always leads to dissatisfaction.

What if you gave your baby sister a great doll that you picked out for
her, and she said, "It's not like the one on television! I want the doll on
television!" How would that make you feel? I'm really disappointed
when you're not satisfied with what I've given you. Don't like your hair
color? Hate your nose? Wish you had someone else's body? I long
for you to be satisfied with your life. I love you the way you are. The
first step to satisfaction is thanking Me for what you have.

Your Loving Father,
>God

== == ==    == == == == == == == == ==

# DON'T HOLD BACK!

**Love the LORD your God with all your heart and with all your soul and with all your strength.**

**Deuteronomy          6:5**

---------------------------------------------

Dear Child,

>I like Mike. Seriously, Michael Jordan is great. I've never seen him hold back on the court. He always goes 100 percent. Even when his team is winning by forty points, Jordan still plays his best.

I want you to be that way with Me. Love Me with everything you have. Love Me with your body—dance, run, play a musical instrument, skateboard, feed hungry people. Love Me with your emotions—cry, yell, laugh, sing. Love Me with your mind—write poetry, solve difficult problems, draw great pictures. I am passionate! Just look at the intense world I made. I don't do anything halfway. It's all or nothing. You be the same way. Go for it!

Your Full-On Creator,
>God

== == ==    == == == == == == == == ==

# GET A LIFE

**The LORD is your life.**

**Deuteronomy 30:20**

-------------------------------------------

My Child,

>I've heard people say, "Music is my life," "My boyfriend is my life," or "Computers are my life." When something is your life, that something means everything to you. Without that something, your life is meaningless.

Who will say, "The Lord is my life"? I am the One who made you, and I made you to know Me. I want to hang out with you. I want to tell you things. I want to be your life. A real relationship with Me is the most amazing thing anyone could ever experience. Yet so many people die without ever knowing Me. Will you let Me be your life? I guarantee that you won't regret it.

The Full Life,
>God

== == ==    == == == == == == == == ==

# LET ME AT 'EM

**One of you routs a thousand, because the Lord
your God fights for you, just as he promised.**

**Joshua          23:10**

---

My Child,

>At the end of every action movie, the good guy is always surrounded
on every side, completely outnumbered by the bad guys. Yet
miraculously, the good guy is always the last one left standing. How
does he do it? Well, it's a movie.

But I can work the same miracles for you. Name your enemies—
anger, depression, addiction, sadness, fear. No matter how many
there are, I will send them running in terror. Remember that I'm God. I
made everything. I can do anything, and I want to fight for you. So
don't be discouraged when it looks like you're outnumbered. Pray,
"Lord, the bad guys are everywhere. I need Your help." I will come to
your rescue. You are not alone in this. I want to help you.

Your Deliverer,
>God

== == ==    == == == == == == == == ==

# YOU CAN'T MAKE ME STOP

**Give thanks to the LORD, for he is good;
his love endures forever.**

**1 Chronicles        16:34**

---------------------------------------------

My Precious Child,

>I'll never stop loving you. No matter what you do, I'll always love
you. If you say you hate Me, I'll still love you. If you disobey Me and
hurt others, I'll love you. If you make mistakes, I'll still love you. If you
become popular and forget all your old friends, I'll still love you.

If all your friends turn on you and say they hate you, I'll still love you.
If you're reading this right now, thinking, *Yeah, sure, right, I doubt it,* I
still love you. The truth is, you can't make Me stop loving you. That's
good news. It means that no matter how bad you've blown it and no
matter how many people have given up on you, I will never give up
on you. My love will always be here for you. I will love you forever.

Your Father,
>God

== == ==    == == == == == == == == ==

# I FEEL YOUR PAIN

**I will be glad and rejoice in your love, for you saw my affliction and knew the anguish of my soul.**

**Psalm          31:7**

---

Dear Child,

>You've heard the phrase, "I feel your pain"? Well, I literally feel your pain. When My Son, Jesus, was on the cross, He felt every evil ever done to anyone. Did a good friend put you down and hurt your feelings last week? Jesus felt it on the cross. Did a relative hurt you physically when you were growing up? Jesus felt it on the cross.

Right now, I know exactly what you are going through. Even if no one else understands, I can see into your heart. When you are down, when it feels like your heart is torn in half, I know. Bring your pain to Me. Tell Me all about it. I will feel sad with you. And in the end, I will take your pain away and give you My joy. I love you so much.

Your Comfort,
>God

== == ==    == == == == == == == == ==

# DO THE RIGHT THING

**The LORD loves righteousness and justice.**

**Psalm         33:5**

-------------------------------------------

My Child,

>You live in a world full of cheaters and liars. Even the best person has lied at one time or another. But I never lie, and I never cheat. I never do anything wrong. I never turn away when someone needs Me. I always stand up for the helpless. I always defend the weak. I always oppose the bullies. I always love. I always do the right thing.

Do you want to be for Me or against Me? If you're against Me, you'll only end up hurting yourself. Whoever cheats or lies or takes advantage of someone's weakness is against Me. In the end, that person will fail. If you're for Me, you will speak up when you see something wrong. If you're for Me, you'll help people who need help— losers, poor people, sad people, unloved people, ugly people. If you're for Me, you'll let Me use you to bring My love into the world. I want to make things right. Will you help Me?

Your Justice,
>God

== == ==    == == == == == == == == ==

# NOT FOR SALE

### How priceless is your unfailing love!

Psalm            36:7

-------------------------------------------

Dear Child,

>Some ancient artifacts and treasures are priceless. No amount of money could buy the pyramids of Egypt. A human life is priceless, which is why I hate slavery. Your parents are priceless. Without them, you wouldn't be here.

You are priceless to Me, and I want My love to be priceless to you. How much would you pay for someone to love and accept you perfectly? How much would you pay for a love that never runs out? How much would you pay to be loved by someone who would always care for you, always watch out for you, and never give up on you, no matter what? My love is priceless, and yet I give it away for free. My love is the most valuable thing in the world. Come get some.

Your Treasure,
>God

== == ==   == == == == == == == == ==

# DON'T KEEP IT A SECRET

**I do not hide your righteousness in my heart;
I speak of your faithfulness and salvation.**

**Psalm          40:10**

-------------------------------------------

My Child,

>One of the best ways to advertise a new product is by word of mouth. If your friends tell you that the new Western Super-Duper Burger is delicious, that means a lot more than any commercial telling you it's really great. Of course the commercial is going to say it's good. They want your money. But if your friends say it's good, they're just telling you what they think.

Have I been faithful to you? Have you found comfort in Me? Do you enjoy Me? Has My love meant anything to you? Then tell your friends about Me. They know you. They will believe you before they will a preacher on TV. Tell your friends about the Bible. Tell them about Jesus and the Cross. Loan them this book. Don't keep Me all to yourself. Spread the word.

Your Good News,
>God

== == ==    == == == == == == == == ==

# NOT YET

**How long must I wrestle with my thoughts and every day have sorrow in my heart? How long will my enemy triumph over me? Look on me and answer, O Lᴏʀᴅ my God.**

**Psalm 13:2-3**

-------------------------------------------

Dear Child,

>Time is a strange thing. To Me, a day is like a thousand years, and a thousand years is like a day. I'm outside of time. Time is just something I made in which you live. I entered time when I sent Jesus to earth. So I know how frustrating time can be.

But I also know what's best for you. The only way you can learn patience is by waiting. Some people pray, "Lord, teach me patience, and teach it to me now!" That doesn't make much sense. Learning patience takes time. I hear your prayers. Keep praying. I may give you an answer quickly, but if I'm teaching you to trust Me no matter what, I may ask you to wait. If you can learn to trust Me, if you can learn to wait on My timing, I will use you to do great things. Will you trust Me?

Your Leader,
>God

== == ==   == == == == == == == == ==

# WATCH YOUR TONGUE

**Though you probe my heart and examine me at night,
though you test me, you will find nothing;
I have resolved that my mouth will not sin.**

**Psalm          17:3**

---------------------------------------------

Dear Child,

>Have you ever been to a fast-food restaurant where the service was terrible? After four or five times of the same slow and terrible service, maybe you vowed, "That's it! I'm never eating at Lazy Burger again!" Were you able to keep your vow? What about when all your friends said, "Let's go eat at Lazy Burger." Did you tell them, "No, I'll never eat there again!"

Some of My children are pretty stubborn. The trick is to use your stubbornness for good. Decide in your heart, "No matter what happens, only positive words will come out of my mouth." That's an oath I'll help you keep. You may have to bite your lip, but if you decide to only speak positive things, I'll help you do it (even in the drive-up line at Lazy Burger!)

Your Helper,
>God

== == ==    == == == == == == == == ==

# I'LL CATCH YOU

**When I said, "My foot is slipping,"
your love, O LORD, supported me.**

**Psalm         94:18**

---------------------------------------------

Dear Child,

>Have you ever been rock climbing? They hook you to a rope on a pulley, and up you climb. The angle is steep, and the rock is jagged. Sometimes the only thing you have to grab on to is a tiny ledge. Until you can figure out where to grab next, you have to hold yourself there by just your fingertips.

Sometimes your foot slips, you lose your grip, or you reach for a handhold that's not really there. That's when you fall. The good news is that you don't fall far, because the rope catches you, and you can start climbing again. It would be crazy, dangerous, and scary to rock climb without a safety rope, because even the best climbers slip and fall. Life is like the rock, and My love is like your rope. Climb well, do your best, and when you can't hang on anymore, My love will hold you up.

Your Support,
>God

== == ==    == == == == == == == == ==

# FRIEND IS AS FRIEND DOES

**I love the LORD, for he heard my voice;
he heard my cry for mercy.**

**Psalm          116:1**

-------------------------------------------

Dear Child,

>Think about your best friend. Did you just decide one day that you were going to make that person your best friend? No, you and your best friend have a history. Maybe one time your best friend called you up, asking for help, and you were able to solve a tough homework problem. Maybe one day at school people were picking on you, and your best friend came to your defense. Your best friend is your best friend because time and time again that person acted like your best friend.

I'm no different. I want to be your best friend if you'll let Me. Call Me up when you're in trouble. Hang out with Me. Let's develop a history together. Then you'll be able to tell people, "God is my best friend," and you'll be able to tell them some reasons why.

Your Friend,
>God

== == ==    == == == == == == == == ==

# WELCOME TO CAMP LIFE

I delight in your commands because I love them.
I lift up my hands to your commands, which
I love, and I meditate on your decrees.

Psalm          119:47-48

---------------------------------------------

My Child,

>Most people hate rules, so why should you love My rules? Well, imagine you're at a camp with no counselors and no rules. Sounds like fun, and maybe it is for a while. Then the bullies start picking on everybody, they eat all the food, and they break everything. Nobody does any cleaning, and pretty soon everything is dirty and gross. How is that fun?

My rules tell you how to do things right. I don't make up rules just to put you down. I make up rules to help you. I'm God. I'm not just a counselor at Camp Life. I built Camp Life. I know where the fun trails are, I know how deep the lake is, and I know which snakes are poisonous and which snakes aren't. So read the Bible and learn My commands. Obey them. Love them. If you will, your life will be a whole lot better.

Your Counselor,
>God

== == ==    == == == == == == == == ==

# KEEP IT TO YOURSELF

**He who covers over an offense promotes love, but whoever repeats the matter separates close friends.**

Proverbs          17:9

------------------------------------------

My Precious Child,

>If one of your friends is mean to you, what should you do? You could forgive your friend and just keep quiet about it. Or you could tell all your other friends how mean that person was to you. But what's the point of blabbing about it? What would you be trying to prove? Nothing. It would just be a way to get even.

Don't stoop to that level. Eventually, that person might notice how nice you are and ask, "Why don't you hate me?" Then you can explain about Me and My ways. Hopefully, your friend will be sorry, and you'll be friends again. Even if your friend isn't sorry, you still don't have to blab to everybody. Treat that person the way you would like to be treated, even if your friend was wrong.

Your Father,
>God

== == ==    == == == == == == == == ==

# HOT MARSHMALLOWS ARE WORTH THE WAIT

**Do not arouse or awaken love until it so desires.**

**Song of      Solomon 8:4**

-------------------------------------------

Dear Child,

>Have you ever roasted marshmallows around a campfire? Imagine that your friends forgot the marshmallows. They tell you, "We're going back to the cabin to get them. We'll be back in an hour." Is that the time to start heaping all the wood on the fire? It might flame up real well for a while, but by the time your friends returned, the fire would be out and you'd all be stuck eating cold marshmallows.

Romantic love is like that fire. Until you're married, it's not time to get all heated up and start making out. It's certainly not yet time for sex. If you save your passion until you get married, you'll have hot marshmallows, and they'll taste wonderful. If you start making out now, you'll only ignite all sorts of confusion and pain. I made sex for marriage. Save it until then.

Your Father,
>God

== == ==    == == == == == == == == ==

# NOW YOU SEE IT—NOW YOU DON'T

**You have put all my sins behind your back.**

**Isaiah        38:17**

---------------------------------------------

Dear Child,

>When a mom catches her child stealing cookies, sometimes the guilty kid will hide the cookies behind his back. But what if the mom took the cookies and hid them behind *her* back? Wow! That would mean: (1) the mom knew about the stolen cookies, (2) the mom was willing to forgive the child for stealing, and (3) the cookie incident was over and forgotten and put behind her.

When you tell Me about your disobedience and ask Me to forgive you, I put your "cookie incident" behind My back. I don't dwell on it or keep beating you up about it. I forget it. So be quick to ask Me for forgiveness. I won't slap you down. I'll cleanse your disobedience so you can start over. That's good news.

Your Forgiver,
>God

== == ==    == == == == == == == == ==

# I'VE ALWAYS LOVED YOU

I have loved you with an everlasting love;
I have drawn you with loving-kindness.

Jeremiah           31:3

---------------------------------------------

My Wonderful Child,

>Did you choose Me, or did I choose you? How did you come to be
reading this book? Why is your head full of thoughts about Me? If you
are a Christian, how did you get to know Me? If you're not a Christian,
why are you so interested in Me?

The answer is simple. Even before you were born, I loved you. And
since the day you were born, I have been drawing you to Myself. I
have been leading and guiding you your whole life. My love is like a
hot, delicious meal. You catch a whiff and follow it to its source. I have
chosen you as My child. Go deeper with Me. Let Me love you more.
Let Me be even more involved with your life.

Your Creator,
>God

== == ==    == == == == == == == == ==

# I DON'T NEED A SHOW

**Rend your heart and not your garments.**

**Joel        2:13**

-------------------------------------------

Dear Child,

>When you apologize to Me about something you've done wrong, I
don't need a big dramatic show. Some people tell Me, "I'm so sorry,
God. I'll never do it again. I'll dress in black for the next two weeks to
prove how sorry I am." I don't care about that kind of outward apology.

I see your heart. If you're really sorry, dress your heart in black. Feel
genuine sorrow. Make things right between yourself and whomever
you may have hurt. Most importantly, do the right thing next time.
Then I'll know that you mean it. Then I will forgive you and help you
do what's right. I don't care whether you're sorry on the outside. It's
the inside that counts.

Your Forgiver,
>God

== == ==    == == == == == == == == ==

# IT'S NOT ALL ABOUT MONEY

**You cannot serve both God and Money.**

Matthew 6:24

---------------------------------------------

My Child,

>Do you trust Me to take care of you, or do you trust in your money?
If you go to college, get a high-paying job, and have a large house
and a fancy car, will that protect you from any problems? No. Things
go wrong, even for rich people. Money can't protect you from everything.

But I *can* protect you—whether you have money or not. I control all
the money in the world. I own everything. It's My world. So why not
rely on Me instead of money. I can give you the money you need, or I
can just give you the things you need without you even having to
spend money on them. The point is that I can take care of you. If you
trust in money to take care of you, eventually it will let you down.

Your Provider,
>God

== == ==    == == == == == == == == ==

# YOU WOULDN'T DO THAT TO YOURSELF

**Love your neighbor as yourself.**

Matthew          22:39

-------------------------------------------

Dear Child,

>Would you hit yourself? Would you lie to yourself? Would you make an appointment with yourself and show up thirty minutes late? Would you tell yourself, "I'll call you tonight," and then never call? Would you be rude to yourself? Would you leave yourself out? Would you ignore yourself?

I want you to love your neighbors as much as you love yourself. Who are your neighbors? The people around you are your neighbors. That means everybody. Wherever you go, all the people you see are your neighbors. I love you, and if you love My Son, you've been adopted into My family. But not everybody knows Me as their Father. So I want you to show all people My love. When they ask, "Why are you being so nice to me?" you can tell them, "Because God told me to. He loves you."

Your Father,
>God

== == ==    == == == == == == == == ==

# LOVE IS A VERB, NOT AN EMOTION

### This is my command: Love each other.

**John          15:17**

--------------------------------------------

My Child,

>Some days, you feel like loving your parents, and some days, you don't. Unfortunately, love isn't an option; it's a commandment. I never said, "Just love people when you feel like it." I said, "Love people whether you feel like it or not."

If I'm mad at you, can I still buy you an ice-cream cone? Sure I can. If you're mad at Me, can you still treat Me with respect? Sure you can. The kind of love I'm commanding here doesn't have anything to do with your feelings. This is not romantic love. The love I'm talking about is a choice; it's something you do. When I say, "Love each other," I mean, "Act lovingly toward each other." If you do, your feelings will eventually come around to match your actions. But don't wait until you feel loving towards someone before you act lovingly towards them.

Your Loving Father,
>God

== == ==    == == == == == == == == ==

# IT'S NOT WHAT YOU KNOW

Knowledge puffs up, but love builds up.

1 Corinthians          8:1

---------------------------------------------

Dear Child,

>Would I rather you know a bunch of things, or would I rather you love people? What do you think? Knowing lots of information is fine, but if all it does is make you conceited, what good is it? You can't impress Me with what you know. Lots of people know lots of things about Me, but where are the people who will love in My name?

Look at the heroes of the Bible. What did they know? Peter was a plain fisherman, the prophet Amos was a farmer, and John the Baptist preached in the desert and ate locusts and wild honey. Even Jesus was a carpenter. It doesn't take a college degree to please Me. If you encourage, help, and care about other people, that impresses Me.

Your Encourager,
>God

== == ==    == == == == == == == == ==

# I SEE YOUR TEARS

**Blessed are those who mourn, for they will be comforted.**

Matthew     5:4

---------------------------------------------

My Child,

>Is it good to be sad? Well, it depends on what you're sad about. If you're sad because you didn't get the latest video game for Christmas, you'll just have to get over it. But what if you're sad because of something more serious? Did a relative die? Do your friends reject you? Do you feel empty inside because someone has seriously hurt you? If so, then yes, you can be blessed by My comforting presence.

If your heart is breaking, My Spirit is with you. I know what's making you sad. I want to make it better. Cry out to Me. Pour your heart out to Me. Ask Me to help you. I will pick you up, dry your tears, and hold you. I will tell you that I love you. I promise I will be with you always.

Your Comfort,
>God

== == ==    == == == == == == == == ==

# NEWS FLASH: YOU'RE NOT THE GREATEST

**Blessed are the meek, for they will inherit the earth.**

**Matthew          5:5**

-------------------------------------------

Dear Child,

>*Meek* does not mean *weak. Meek* means *gentle.* There's a big difference. A meek person might be stronger than the strongest wrestler or smarter than the smartest scientist. But a meek person doesn't use that strength to put other people down.

Proud athletes brag and boast when they win a championship. "I am the greatest," one famous boxer always used to say. But meek champions thank their teammates, their coach, and their fans. If you brag about yourself and hog the spotlight, that's your reward. But if you are meek and give the glory to others, I will give you a reward far greater than a trophy or fame. I will give you a place of honor in My kingdom, because I know you can be trusted.

Your Fan,
>God

== == ==    == == == == == == == == ==

# JUSTICE IS COMING

**Blessed are those who hunger and thirst for righteousness, for they will be filled.**

Matthew            5:6

------------------------------------------

My Child,

>Why do bad things happen to good people? Why do good things happen to bad people? Sometimes it seems like the world is upside down. Drug dealers have lots of money, and honest workers struggle to make ends meet. Mean people are popular, and nice people are left out. Do these things bother you? Good. That means you hunger for righteousness.

I am a righteous God. The reason I don't fix everything right now is that I'm giving the bad guys a chance to change. Jesus died so that everybody could know Me, even drug dealers and mean people. So I'm waiting for them to come to Me. But I won't wait forever. Soon, I'm coming back to make everything right, and those who laughed at Me won't be laughing anymore. A time of justice is coming. Until then, do the right thing yourself, and pray for righteousness in the world.

Your Righteousness,
>God

== == ==    == == == == == == == == ==

# THE LOVE PROPELLER

**Christ's love compels us.**

**2 Corinthians      5:14**

---------------------------------------------

Dear Child,

>What drives you? What motivates you? What inspires you? Are you driven to make good grades? Are you driven to be popular? Are you driven to excel in sports? More than any of those things, I want My Son's love to motivate you.

Jesus was propelled by His love for you. He loved you so much that He let evil men torture and crucify Him, just so you could have a relationship with Him. Jesus loves you so much He prays for you all the time. He sends His angels to watch over you. Since Jesus loves you so much, let His love prompt you to tell others about Him. Let His love challenge you to obey Him. Most importantly, let His love encourage you to love Him back. If you are moved by Jesus' love for you, then you will live an amazing life.

Your Motivation,
>God

== == ==    == == == == == == == == ==

# SHOW ME THE MONEY

**See that you also excel in this grace of giving.**

**2 Corinthians      8:7**

-------------------------------------------

My Child,

>Do you get excited about giving money and gifts away? It may sound crazy, but giving away money is something I want you to enjoy. Do you have a friend who needs some cheering up? Go ahead and buy your friend that new CD he's been wanting.

The secret to giving is realizing that I created all the wealth in the world. When you give a gift, you're just shifting My money to someone else. And don't be surprised if a little while later, some of My money gets shifted back to you. Once you realize that it's not your money, giving becomes fun. Ask Me right now to show you someone who needs something. Listen and go bless that person. There's nothing more exciting than being used by Me to meet someone else's need.

Your Provider,
>God

== == ==    == == == == == == == == ==

# WHAT WOULD THEY SAY?

**Live a life of love.**

**Ephesians          5:2**

---------------------------------------------

My Child,

>If you died tonight, how would you be remembered? At your funeral, what would they say? Would they say, "That person loved to win," or, "That person really loved baseball"? Would they say, "Oh yeah, I think that person went to church once in a while"?

Or would it be different? Would someone stand up and say, "She was kind to me my first day at school. When everyone else ignored me, she asked me to sit with her at lunch. I'll always remember that." Will someone else say, "She always encouraged me to hang in there at track practice. I ran my best race because of her."

Are you living a life of love that is making a real difference, or are you living a life that hardly matters? When everything else fades away, the love you show to others is what will last. So live a life of love.

The One Who Loves You,
>God

== == ==    == == == == == == == == ==

# STOP BRAGGING AND LOVE SOMEBODY

**If anyone says, "I love God," yet hates his brother, he is a liar. For anyone who does not love his brother, whom he has seen, cannot love God, whom he has not seen.**

**1 John          4:20**

---------------------------------------------

Dear Child,

>What if some guy in your English class was always talking about how much he loved writing and how great he was at it? "I've had novels published in Europe," he boasts. "My writing is quite popular in New York City." However, if he never turned in any of his writing assignments and received an "F" for the class, would you believe his bragging? No way!

Now what if some woman at your church is always talking about how much she loves Me. "God is my everything," she says. "I've read all the books of the Bible." But if she never loves or helps anybody and never listens to anyone else, would you believe her? Me neither. Don't be like that. If you want to love Me, love other people. That's how I'll know you're serious about Me.

Your Lord,
>God

== == ==    == == == == == == == == ==

# DON'T IGNORE THE SPANKING

**Those whom I love I rebuke and discipline.
So be earnest, and repent.**

**Revelation          3:19**

---------------------------------------------

My Dear Child,

>If I didn't care about you, I would just say, "Yep, My child's messing up again. That kid will never learn." But since I do care about you, I'm going to get involved. If you keep messing up, I'm going to correct you. I'm going to point out your mistakes and help you fix them. It might even feel like I'm giving you a spiritual spanking. It doesn't mean I hate you; it means I love you enough to get involved.

When you feel My discipline, don't ignore it. That will only make your life worse. Instead, admit your mistakes, get serious about the problem, and ask Me to help you fix it. Please understand that I could never hate you, even when you do wrong. I will always love you.

Your Loving Father,
>God

== == ==    == == == == == == == == ==

# THERE'S PLENTY MORE WHERE THAT CAME FROM

**May the Lord make your love increase and overflow for each other and for everyone else.**

1 Thessalonians        3:12

-------------------------------------------

Dear Child,

>You can't have too much love. It's not like too much candy that makes you sick. If fifty people in a school are full of love, that school will be a good place to attend. If a hundred people in a school are full of love, that school will be even better.

As God, I have an infinite supply of love. I am love, and I never run out. Ask Me, and I will pour out so much love on you, you won't be able to keep it to yourself. You will have to share it. It will literally overflow from you to other people. Do you want your life to overflow with love? Ask Me to fill you with a double portion, and watch what happens. You can't have too much love.

The Original Love Connection,
>God

== == ==    == == == == == == == == ==

# MAYBE IT'S TIME FOR A CHANGE

**Flee the evil desires of youth, and pursue righteousness, faith, love and peace, along with those who call on the Lord out of a pure heart.**

**2 Timothy          2:22**

---------------------------------------------

Dear Child,

>You may be wondering, "What are the evil desires of youth?" Drinking, drugs, rebellion, sex, gossip, laziness, and anger are just a few. You should run away from those things. Evil desires are like a roaring lion. Sooner or later, if you give in to them, they will chew you up and spit you out. You wouldn't just run headlong and throw yourself at a roaring lion, would you?

Maybe all your friends are running towards evil. In that case, you probably need to switch friends. There is an army full of kids your age who are following Me, obeying Me, and turning from evil. You can find them at churches and even at your school. If you feel like you're the only one in your group who cares about Me, join another group.

Your Leader,
>God

== == ==    == == == == == == == == ==

# GET A JOB

**God is not unjust; he will not forget your work and
the love you have shown him as you have
helped his people and continue to help them.**

**Hebrews 6:10**

---------------------------------------------

My Dear Child,

>There's nothing worse than working hard for a boss or a teacher and not receiving any recognition or appreciation. I'm not like that. I see every good thing you do, and I appreciate it. A good way to work for Me is to help other Christians do their jobs.

There are Christians at churches all over your city who are working to share My love. Some churches are feeding hungry people. Other churches are going into the streets to tell people about My love. Other churches are visiting sick people in the hospital and praying for them to be healed. You don't have to make up something new to do for Me. You can just join a group that's already doing something for Me. Ask around and see where you can be most helpful. I won't forget the work you do for Me. I appreciate you.

Your Heavenly Boss,
>God

== == ==    == == == == == == == == ==

# GIVE ME A "G"! GIVE ME AN "O"!

**Let us consider how we may spur one another on toward love and good deeds.**

**Hebrews        10:24**

-------------------------------------------

My Child,

>Why do teams have cheerleaders? The cheerleaders are supposed to get the crowds to cheer. When the players get discouraged, they hear the crowds yelling and think, *We can still win this thing. All these people are pulling for us.* Why do boxers have trainers in their corners? So that in between rounds, when the boxer limps back to his corner tired and discouraged, the trainer can yell, "Keep your hands up! Hit him in the ribs! Stay on your toes! You're the champ!"

Encouragement can mean the difference between winning and losing. So encourage your friends to keep doing the right thing. Maybe an appreciative note or a Bible verse will encourage them. Maybe telling them how great they are will build them up. Maybe just listening will make the difference. But whatever it takes, do it. Later when you're discouraged, I hope your friends will encourage you.

Your Encourager,
>God

== == ==    == == == == == == == == ==

# ANGER WILL BE THE DEATH OF YOU

**We know that we have passed from death to life, because we love our brothers. Anyone who does not love remains in death.**

1 John          3:14

---

My Child,

>Have you ever been so mad that you couldn't forgive? Try to remember how it felt. Did your unforgiveness feel good? Were you peaceful and relaxed as you hated that other person's guts? When you can't forgive someone, when you can't love someone, you become dead to all the other good things in life.

When you are full of anger, you have no life. You don't smile. You're not excited about anything. You can't relax. You have a big knot in your stomach because of what that other person did to you. All you can think about is how you're going to get even. That's no way to live. Is there anyone in your life that you hate that much? Forgive them, let it go, and start living again.

Your Forgiver,
>God

== == ==    == == == == == == == == ==

# HOW MUCH DO YOU REALLY NEED?

**If anyone has material possessions and sees his brother in need but has no pity on him, how can the love of God be in him?**

**1 John          3:17**

---------------------------------------------

My Child,

>I didn't put you on earth so that you could collect a bunch of stuff. I don't mind you using the things I've given you to take care of yourself. It's okay to own a coat. It's good to own shoes. I don't even mind you enjoying the extra things I've given you, like televisions and video games and CDs. But if you have an extra jacket, and you see another person who needs one, give your extra jacket away.

Trust Me to meet your needs. I can give you another jacket. Maybe the person in need isn't a Christian. Maybe he doesn't know Me or trust Me. Maybe I'm using you to show that person that I still care. Here's the general rule: If you have something that you don't need, and somebody else needs it, pass it on.

Your Provider,
>God

== == ==    == == == == == == == == ==

# MY LOVE IS THE BEST

**This is love: not that we loved God, but that he loved us and sent his Son as an atoning sacrifice for our sins.**

1 John          4:10

-------------------------------------------

My Dear Child,

>If you want to know what your new neighbor looks like, is it better to look at a drawing of him or go meet him in person? The original is always better than the copy. If you want to know what love looks like, don't look at human love, look at My love. Human beings can only love because I put My love in them. Human love is the copy, but My love is the original.

Human love is imperfect. People get impatient, they're selfish, and they break their commitments. But My love is perfect. It never changes. It lasts in the good times and in the bad. If you want to see a great example of love, look at My Son Jesus who suffered on the cross so that you could be in My family. That's intense love. It doesn't get any better than that.

The Source of Love,
>God

== == ==    == == == == == == == == ==

# TAKE A CHANCE

**We know and rely on the love God has for us.**

1 John                    4:16

-------------------------------------------

Dear Child,

>Have you ever gone hiking with a walking stick? It makes hiking a lot easier. You don't even have to lean on it all the time; just knowing it's there makes you more confident. With a walking stick, you will take risks on a steep trail that you wouldn't otherwise.

I want My love for you to be like that walking stick. I love you so much, and I will never stop loving you. I want you to know My love and rely on it. Just knowing that I love you should give you confidence to risk being rejected by people, because My love will catch you if they hurt you. You can afford to take chances. You can afford to love the unlovable. No matter what happens, you can never lose My love.

Your Support,
>God

== == ==    == == == == == == == == ==

# FINISH STRONG

**I have brought you glory on earth by
completing the work you gave me to do.**

**John          17:4**

---------------------------------------------

Dear Child,

>It matters how you start a race, but the most important thing is how
you finish it. At the start of a cross-country race, lots of people run
ahead, full of fresh energy. But three miles later, many of those early
leaders are nowhere to be seen. They started strong, but they didn't
finish strong.

You be one who finishes strong. Pace yourself. Look at your life and
see what it's going to take to finish the best you can. Should you go
to college? Should you be a missionary? Whatever you do, don't just
do it with the short term in mind. Live your whole life as if you are
running a race for Me, because you are. Then at the end of your life,
you will be able to join Jesus in saying, "Father, I did what You told
me to do. I finished strong."

Your Goal,
>God

== == ==    == == == == == == == == ==

# I KNOW WHAT YOU DID LAST SUMMER (AND LAST NIGHT!)

**Woe to those who go to great depths to hide their plans from the LORD, who do their work in darkness and think, "Who sees us? Who will know?"**

Isaiah          29:15

---------------------------------------------

Dear Child,

>I know everything. You should realize that about Me. I know everything you've done, and I also know everything you've thought. So if you plan on doing something without Me knowing about it, you're fooling yourself. I know you better than you know yourself.

If you told a secret you promised to keep, and then you come praying to Me this morning, "Oh, Lord. Good morning. I worship You today," I'll be thinking, *Really? What about the secret you revealed?* So don't come praying to Me like I don't know what you've done. Tell me what you've done, apologize, plan not to do it again, and then you can pray honestly. I already know everything anyway. I just want us to be honest with each other. Okay?

The All-Knowing,
>God

== == ==    == == == == == == == == ==

# DON'T EXPECT A PARADE

**Consider him who endured such opposition from
sinful men, so that you will not grow weary and lose heart.**

**Hebrews        12:3**

------------------------------------------

My Child,

>When you stand up for what's right, some people aren't going to like
it. My Son, Jesus, stood against greed when He drove the merchants
out of the temple, and the merchants hated Him for cutting into their
profits. Jesus stood against prejudice when He ate at a tax collector's
house, and the prejudiced religious people hated Him for it.

When you are good to others, the people who are mean aren't going
to like you much, because your good behavior is a criticism of their
bad behavior. But don't let that stop you. Later, some of your enemies
may admire your courage and change their minds. But don't expect
everyone to shout for joy because you're following Me. That's okay.
Don't take it personally. Plenty of people didn't like Jesus either. It
comes with the territory.

Your Encourager,
>God

== == ==    == == == == == == == == ==

# PUT YOUR TREASURE WHERE YOUR HEART IS

**Where your treasure is, there your heart will be also.**

Matthew          6:21

---------------------------------------------

My Child,

>Once upon a time, a rich man named Mr. Smith spent hundreds of thousands of dollars restoring a fancy antique car. Every chance he had, he was in his garage fixing the car, polishing it, or making adjustments to its engine. When he took the car out for a drive, people would say, "Here comes Mr. Smith in his baby." He loved that car so much, people thought of it as his child. Mr. Smith spent his treasure—his time, energy, and money—on his car, and that's where his heart was, too.

Unlike Mr. Smith, I want you to spend your treasure on Me. I don't mind if you have other interests, but don't make them your life. Spend your time getting to know Me. Spend your money on the work I am doing in the world. Spend your mind learning about Me and My Bible. Spend your creativity making art that celebrates Me. Spend your energy loving people in My name. Your treasure will be waiting for you here in Heaven, because I will be your treasure.

Your Reward,
>God

== == ==    == == == == == == == == ==

# JUST BELIEVE

**I tell you the truth, if anyone says to this mountain, "Go, throw yourself into the sea," and does not doubt in his heart but believes that what he says will happen, it will be done for him.**

**Mark          11:23**

-------------------------------------------

Dear Child,

>Do you believe that I can do anything? Do you believe that I want to help you? If you answered yes to both of those questions, then you are ready to pray with faith. Do you have a difficult test coming up at school, one you don't think you can pass? Can I help you pass it? Yes. Do I want to help you pass it? Yes. So what's the game plan?

Pray like this, "God, I believe You can do anything. Please help me pass this test. Thank You. I believe You are going to help me." Then go study. Now if you haven't paid attention in class and you haven't read the chapter, I won't have as much to work with, and you probably will not do well. When you do your part, I can help you be successful. Don't doubt. Just believe. Those who believe in Me are the ones who see My miracles.

Your Helper,
>God

== == ==    == == == == == == == == ==

# FOR YOUR EARS ONLY

**Mary treasured up all these things and pondered them in her heart.**

**Luke 2:19**

---------------------------------------------

My Dear Child,

>Do you know how to keep a secret? Think about Mary. Right after she gives birth to Jesus, all these excited shepherds show up in the middle of the night. "We just saw a ton of angels, and they said your baby was going to save the entire world!" Wow! Wouldn't you want to share that news with your friends?

But Mary didn't tell anybody. She just kept it to herself and thought about it. Way to go, Mary! When you pray, sometimes I will tell you specific things that are just for you. It might be good news about your future. It might be a promise. It might just be Me telling you why I like you. I have secrets that I want to share with only you, but I have to be able to trust you not to blab them to everyone. Can you keep a secret?

Your Best Friend,
>God

== == ==    == == == == == == == == ==

# THEY WILL PUT YOU DOWN

**Blessed are those who are persecuted because of righteousness, for theirs is the kingdom of heaven.**

**Matthew      5:10**

-------------------------------------------

Dear Child,

>When you obey and follow Me, eventually you will be persecuted. Persecution isn't only physical abuse. When people put you down for doing the right thing, that's persecution, too. There are lots of people in this world who have chosen to go against Me. When you obey Me, your obedience will bother My enemies, and they will put you down.

When you love people, when you take up for the kids called geeks and losers, when you refuse to smoke or drink just because everyone else is doing it, some people won't like it. But when they laugh at you for obeying Me, you are blessed. Why? Because it shows Me that you care more about Me than you do about following the crowd. It shows Me that you are living for Heaven. Good for you. Heaven is waiting for you, and I am proud to call you My child.

Your Proud Father,
>God

== == ==    == == == == == == == == ==

# MUTINY AT THE TOY FACTORY!

**You turn things upside down, as if the potter were thought
to be like the clay! Shall what is formed say to him
who formed it, "He did not make me"?
Can the pot say of the potter, "He knows nothing"?**

Isaiah          29:16

---------------------------------------------

Dear Child,

>Imagine a toy factory where all the toys come to life one night and
decide they must have made themselves. The next morning when the
toy makers come into work, they find a note:

Dear Toy Makers,

You did not make us. We don't need you. We have gone into the
world to seek our fortune.

Signed,
The Toys

It might make a good cartoon movie, but it would never actually happen.
It's silly to even think about. That's how silly it is to Me when humans
say, "There is no God." I remember making the first man. I designed
him. I built him. I breathed life into him. And now My own creation is
telling Me, "You don't exist. We just evolved." Don't you believe it!

Your Maker,
>God

== == ==    == == == == == == == == ==

# LEAN ON ME

**You brought me out of the womb; you made me trust in you even at my mother's breast.**

Psalm                    22:9

-------------------------------------------

My Child,

>Why are human beings born into the world as babies? Why aren't they born fully grown? Colts get up and walk the day they are born. So why are humans born so helpless? One reason is, I want you to understand from the beginning that you are not in control. When you were a newborn, you couldn't feed yourself, you couldn't sit up, and you could barely even see. Without your parents, you would have quickly died.

Now that you aren't a baby anymore, there are lots of things you can do on your own, but I still want you to trust Me. Compared to Me, you are still just a child . . . My child. So rely on Me to supply your needs. When things are too difficult for you, pray and ask for help. You don't have to do it all by yourself. I don't expect you to. You're never too old to depend on Me.

Your Father,
>God

== == ==    == == == == == == == == ==

# MY ANGEL PROTECTS YOU

**The angel of the Lᴏʀᴅ encamps around
those who fear Him, and rescues them.**

**Psalm          34:7 ɴᴀsʙ**

-------------------------------------------

Dear Child,

>When you were a little kid, did your mom ever let you put up a
blanket like a tent in the backyard? Maybe you ate hot dogs, cookies,
and potato chips and read comic books with a flashlight. Everything
was cool as long as you and your friend were laughing and talking.
But when you quieted down, the noises of the night closed in on you,
and it got pretty scary.

Maybe right now the realities of your life are closing in on you just
like those night noises did way back then. I want to reassure you. I
am here. Please don't feel afraid. You are Mine. My power encircles
and defends you. My angels encamp around you and rescue you.
Trust Me.

Your Defense,
>God

== == ==    == == == == == == == == ==

# DON'T FLIP A COIN. PRAY!

## Commit your way to the Lord.

**Psalm**      37:5

---------------------------------------

Dear Child,

>There are several different ways that your life could turn out. You could get into computers and write a piece of software that no one's ever thought of before. You could study acting or music or art. You could major in education and become a college professor who affects hundreds of young lives.

So how do you know which way is the right way for your life? You don't. But I do. So as you make decisions in life, pray, "Lord, which way should I go?" Once you've decided, pray again, "Lord, I believe this is the way You want me to go. Please guide me. If You want to redirect me, I'm open to that." Are you facing a major decision like what sport you should play or which college you should attend? If you ask Me to help you decide, I will always put you on the right path.

Your Guide,
>God

== == ==    == == == == == == == == ==

# DON'T BE A CHANNEL-CHANGER

**Blessed are the pure in heart, for they will see God.**

Matthew        5:8

-------------------------------------------

My Precious Child,

>If something is pure, that means it's 100 percent one thing. Pure gold is not 50 percent gold and 50 percent iron. It's 100 percent gold. Likewise, a pure heart is not 50 percent selfishness and 50 percent love. It's 100 percent love. Your heart is the center of who you are. (I'm not talking about your blood-pumping muscle; I'm talking about the heart of your soul.) I want the deepest part of who you are to be 100 percent devoted to Me.

Have you ever tried to watch a football game and a basketball game at the same time on the same TV? It doesn't really work. You wind up missing the best parts of both games. It's the same way in your relationship with Me. If you are 50 percent devoted to Me and 50 percent devoted to being popular, your heart will be divided and you will miss the best parts of Me. But if your heart is 100 percent devoted to Me, you will see Me in all My glory.

Your Focus,
>God

== == ==    == == == == == == == == ==

# TALK IS CHEAP

**All hard work brings a profit, but
mere talk leads only to poverty.**

**Proverbs          14:23**

--------------------------------------------

Dear Child,

>Have you heard the saying, "Put your money where your mouth is"?
It means, "Stop talking and do something about it." Everybody has
ideas. But not everybody acts on those ideas. Lots of people had
ideas for computer programs in the 1970s, but Bill Gates didn't just
talk about writing computer programs, he sold his computer programs
to IBM.

It's not the talkers who succeed, it's the doers. The same is true when it
comes to following Me. Anybody can sit around and talk about how
much they love Me. But the people who impress Me are the ones who
take action. So tell people about Me, write songs to Me, and work for
Me. Anybody can say they love Me, but will you do something about it?

Your Motivation,
>God

== == ==    == == == == == == == == ==

# THREE, TWO, ONE. . . .

**Man, despite his riches, does not endure;**
**he is like the beasts that perish.**

**Psalm          49:12**

---------------------------------------------

My Child,

>Everybody dies. No matter how rich you are, you will still die. You
can't bribe death. No matter how good-looking you are, you will still
grow old and die. You can't charm death. No matter how smart you
are, you will still get old and die. You can't outsmart death.

Why am I telling you this? Do I want to make you depressed? No, I
just want to make you think. You only have so many years on this
planet, and then you're gone. Those are the facts of life. So make the
most of your time. Don't waste your time hiding from Me and
disobeying Me. Don't waste your time hiding your feelings and playing
it safe. If you were to die tonight, what would you want to tell your
friends and family? Whom would you tell, "I love you"? Go tell them
now, because life is short.

Your Life Giver,
>God

== == ==    == == == == == == == == ==

# GOD LOVES A WORKER

**Jesus said to them, "My Father is always at his work to this very day, and I, too, am working."**

**John          5:17**

--------------------------------------------

My Child,

>I am a working guy. I built the world in six days. I took one day off to rest, and I've been working ever since. My Son, Jesus, is also a working man. He worked as a carpenter for years, and then He became the hardest-working preacher and teacher ever. Jesus and I are still at work. We haven't stopped.

Day and night, I am at work introducing Myself to people who don't know Me. I control the course of governments. I keep the planets spinning. And I work through Christians, doing miracles, healing hearts, and bringing joy into the world. Will you join in and work with Me? You won't have to do the miracles yourself. I will work them through you. You just have to be willing to pray for the people I show to you. If you're interested, pray right now, "Yes, Lord, I will work with You." Then keep your eyes open for your next job assignment.

Your Heavenly Boss,
>God

== == ==    == == == == == == == == ==

# LIKE IT SAYS ON THE MONEY

**Do not put your trust in princes,
in mortal men, who cannot save.**

**Psalm          146:3**

--------------------------------------------

Dear Child,

>Some people are consumed with politics. They believe that once
they elect President So-and-So, everything will be better. I don't mind
if you get involved in politics, but if you're looking to an elected official
to change the world, you are looking in the wrong place.

Don't trust in any man or woman to fix the world. Trust in Me.
Governments can pass all the laws they want, but only I can change
someone's heart. I change people from the inside out, one at a time. I
don't change them with traffic signs and rifles and social programs, I
change them with love. So vote for the best candidate and pray for your
leaders, but trust in Me. The people who formed the United States
government long ago would tell you the same thing. Just take out a
dollar bill and read what it says on the back: "IN GOD WE TRUST."

Your King,
>God

== == ==    == == == == == == == == ==

# FISHING 101

**Trust in the LORD with all your heart and
lean not on your own understanding.**

**Proverbs          3:5**

-------------------------------------------

Dear Child,

>When modern fishermen go deep-sea fishing, they use electronic
depth-finders to help them locate schools of fish. Without a depth-
finder, a fisherman could use his eyes to look into the water, but deep
water is choppy and dark. What looks like a school of fish might only
be a shadow. It's much more reliable for them to use the depth-finder.

I am your depth-finder. You can't figure out everything in life by
yourself, because it's just too confusing. Your reasoning will only get
you so far. There are some problems you'll never figure out. But I
know the solution to every problem. So involve Me in your decision
making. Rely on Me. Pray to Me. Use Me to guide you. I will keep you
off the rocks and steer you into rich waters.

Your Wisdom,
>God

== == ==   == == == == == == == == ==

# THE DISCOVERY CHANNEL

**How many are your works, O L**ORD**! In wisdom you made them all; the earth is full of your creatures.**

**Psalm          104:24**

-------------------------------------------

My Dear Child,

>Do you want to know what I'm like? Just check out some of the animals I have created. A platypus lives half its time in the water and half on land. It lays eggs like a snake, but it gives milk like a mammal. What does a platypus tell you about Me? You can't put Me in a box. I am much bigger than your organized categories. I will always surprise you.

Check out a parrot. Each species of parrot has its own different combination of bright colors on its wings, beak, tail, and feet. And parrots can imitate human speech. What does a parrot tell you about Me? I am wild. I am creative. I am fun. I have a sense of humor. I'm saying, "Don't take yourself so seriously."

These are just two of My creatures out of thousands. Spend some time examining My creation in detail, and you'll discover all sorts of things about Me.

Your Creator,
>God

== == ==    == == == == == == == == ==

# THIS IS NOT THE END

**Let him who walks in the dark, who has no light, trust in the name of the LORD and rely on his God.**

Isaiah          50:10

\-\-\-\-\-\-\-\-\-\-\-\-\-\-\-\-\-\-\-\-\-\-\-\-\-\-\-\-\-\-\-\-\-\-\-\-\-\-\-\-\-\-\-\-

Precious Child,

>Do you sometimes feel like things are closing in on you, and you just can't see? Maybe you've had a terrible week. You're in trouble with your parents again, you're failing science class, or you weren't invited to your friend's party. Whatever it is, when you feel like everything is dark and there's no hope in sight, that's a great time to turn to Me.

My Son, Jesus, has been where you've been . . . and worse. All His friends left Him. He was falsely accused and arrested. He was tortured and nailed to a cross. As Jesus hung there on the cross, things looked hopeless for Him. But three days later, Jesus rose from the dead, and now He's alive and happy. Jesus made it through His darkest time, and He's there to lead you through your difficult times. Just pray, "Jesus, help me. I feel awful." He knows what to do. I love you so much. Hang in there.

Your Way Out,
>God

== == ==     == == == == == == == == ==

# CHURCH IS GREAT, BUT . . .

**Do not trust in deceptive words and say, "This is the temple of the Lord, the temple of the Lord, the temple of the Lord!"**

**Jeremiah          7:4**

-------------------------------------------

Dear Child,

>Going to church is great, but going to church won't get you into Heaven. There are plenty of people who sat in church their whole lives but who ended up in hell. Why? Because they never knew Me. They never asked My Son, Jesus, to rule their lives. Maybe they heard the words of the Bible. Maybe they even fed some street people or went on a mission trip to another country. But as good as those things are, they won't buy you a ticket to Heaven. Knowing Jesus and Me—that's the ticket!

I want so much for you to know Me. If you don't have a real relationship with Me during the week, you will just be going through the motions at church on Sunday. Going to church without knowing Me is like going to a restaurant and reading the menu, but never eating any of the food. What's the point? I don't just want you to know *about* Me. I want you to *know* Me.

Your Lord,
>God

== == ==    == == == == == == == == ==

# 100 PERCENT GOODNESS

**The LORD is good.**

**Nahum** **1:7**

-------------------------------------------

Dear Child,

>Sometimes people ask, "If God is good, then why is there evil in the world?" Hey, evil isn't My fault. I have never done anything evil. People choose to rebel and do evil on their own. Sure, I could end all evil in the world right now, but that would mean taking away your free will. You would be like a puppet, and I would be the puppet master, just pulling your strings. Do you want that? I don't think so. Your love means so much more to Me because you give it freely.

I hate evil. I only put up with it now so that bad people will have a chance to change. But in a little while, I will come and judge all evil. I am totally good. Everything I do is good. Everything I think is good. Every part of Me is good. And I only want to do good to you. If someone has done evil to you, I had nothing to do with it. I will never be anything but good to you.

Your Source of Good,
>God

== == ==   == == == == == == == == ==

# YOU CAN'T KNOW IT ALL

**As you do not know the path of the wind, or how the body is formed in a mother's womb, so you cannot understand the work of God, the Maker of all things.**

**Ecclesiastes          11:5**

---------------------------------------------

My Child,

>You will never totally figure Me out. Don't even try. I've done things and thought things and been things that would literally blow your mind. As long as you live on earth, you will only know Me in part, but that is enough. How can you know Me at all? Because I came down to your level and showed you who I am.

If someone speaks three different languages, and you only speak one language, that person will choose your language and use it to speak to you. Otherwise, how could you understand what's being said? That's what I did when I sent Jesus to earth. I sent Him speaking the language of humanity. I sent Him dressed in human flesh and blood and bones so you could relate to Him. Through Jesus, I brought My unknowable self into a knowable form that you could understand. Everything I want you to know about Me you can learn from Jesus. If you can't learn it from Jesus, you don't need to know it. So get to know Jesus, and you'll know who I am.

Your Infinite Father,
>God

== == ==     == == == == == == == == ==

# DON'T TRASH IT

**If you have not been trustworthy with someone else's property, who will give you property of your own?**

Luke          16:12

-------------------------------------------

My Child,

>Do you want your own car, your own room, your own computer, your own job? Then start by taking care of what you do have. If you leave your bicycle in the middle of the road and it gets run over, that shows Me you don't care about your stuff. So why would I give you more stuff? Just so you can trash it, too? No way.

The same goes for privileges. Do you want to be in a Christian rock band? Then start by being nice to your little brother. If you can't even love the people around you, why would I send you out to love people you don't even know? If you'll take care of the things and the responsibilities you already have, I will give you more.

Your Rewarder,
>God

== == ==    == == == == == == == == ==

# GET GOOD AT IT

**Do you see a man skilled in his work? He will serve before kings; he will not serve before obscure men.**

**Proverbs          22:29**

--------------------------------------------

My Child,

>Honestly, I am tired of people who don't know Me producing all the great works of art. There was a time a few hundred years ago when My people created the majority of the great masterpieces. What happened? Why did Christians stop painting, sculpting, inventing, designing, acting, writing poems, and composing music for the world?

I want you to learn a skill and get good at it: plumbing, carpentry, architecture, dog training, cooking, web-site design, dancing, or management. Discover My plan for your life. Develop your gifts. If you are skilled at what you do, people will respect and listen to you. And while you have their attention, you can tell them about Me. So find something you enjoy doing, and learn how to do it well.

Your Creator,
>God

== == ==    == == == == == == == == ==

# IT'S A MANUAL, NOT A FAIRY TALE

**The one who hears my words and does not put them into practice is like a man who built a house on the ground without a foundation. The moment the torrent struck that house, it collapsed and its destruction was complete.**

**Luke            6:49**

--------------------------------------------

Dear Child,

>Once upon a time, a lawyer went out of town for a week and left his assistant in charge. The lawyer gave his assistant a list of specific instructions. "Can you handle this?" the lawyer asked.

"No problem," the assistant assured him. "I'll take care of it."

A week later, the lawyer returned to total chaos. Nobody was working, and nothing on the list had been done. Furious, the lawyer demanded of his assistant, "What's going on here!"

"Oh," the assistant said, "that list you left us was great. We studied it and talked about it. Some of us even memorized parts of it."

"But did you do any of it?" asked the lawyer.

"Do it? Were we supposed to do it?"

I think you get the idea. The words in My Bible will change your life, but only if you do what they say. Don't just read My Bible. Do what it says.

Your Instructor,
>God

== == ==    == == == == == == == == ==

# IT'S OKAY, YOUR DADDY'S HERE

**Comfort, comfort my people, says your God.**

Isaiah          40:1

---------------------------------------------

My Child,

>Have you ever seen a little kid slip and skin a knee? Hopefully, a parent is nearby to scoop up that child and say, "Daddy's here," or, "Mommy's here. It's okay." The older a child gets, the more society says it's not okay to cry. Teenagers are supposed to act cool. Adults are supposed to hide their hurts.

The problem is, everyone still gets hurt and wants to be comforted. But because people have learned to act like they're fine when they're not, they are full of hidden wounds and silent tears. I want you to know that I see your pain and I care. I am waiting to scoop you up and comfort you. I'm waiting to say, "It's okay, your Daddy's here."

Your Comforter,
>God

== == ==    == == == == == == == == ==

# YOU STILL NEED A SHEPHERD

**He tends his flock like a shepherd: He gathers the lambs
in his arms and carries them close to his heart;
he gently leads those that have young.**

**Isaiah        40:11**

-------------------------------------------

Dear Child,

>If you live in a city, you may not know much about sheep or
shepherds. Let Me fill you in. Sheep are not self-sufficient. If a sheep
falls over in a rainstorm, he'll drown because the rain is falling into his
mouth and nose, and he doesn't even know how to turn himself back
over. That's why a shepherd has to keep a close watch, constantly
protecting his sheep from dangers—like taking a wrong path or being
attacked by larger animals.

Now I'm not saying you're incompetent. I'm proud of the way you're
learning to take care of yourself. But trust Me, you still need a
shepherd. You need someone to help you steer clear of the wrong
paths and the dangerous situations that can trip you up. I'm here
when you need Me. Just ask.

Your Shepherd,
>God

== == ==    == == == == == == == == ==

# WHO'S THE MAN?

**If anyone comes to me and does not hate his father and mother, his wife and children, his brothers and sisters—yes, even his own life—he cannot be my disciple.**

Luke                14:26

-------------------------------------------

My Child,

>Would you choose Me over your parents? Would you choose Me over your friends? Would you risk your life if I asked you to? How important am I to you? Am I something extra tacked on to your life, or am I the purpose of your life? These are hard questions, but I'm asking them of you.

You would not exist without Me and neither would your friends or parents. The world would not exist without Me. Just think: no malls, no grocery stores, no sky, no land, nothing. I am not just a good idea or the teacher of a good way to live your life. I am the One who made your world. I am the One who made you. Give Me your whole life, and I'll give you back such a life of adventure that you could never have imagined it in your wildest dreams. Trust Me, I'm worth it all.

I Am,
>God

== == ==    == == == == == == == == ==

# I'LL BUILD SPIRITUAL MUSCLE IN YOU

**He gives strength to the weary and increases the power of the weak.**

Isaiah          40:29

---------------------------------------------

Dear Child,

>Do you ever feel like a spiritual wimp? Do you find it hard to take a stand and stick to it? Do you vow to do something (or not to do something), fully intending to follow through on your decision, and the next thing you know, you're backing down?

I can give you muscles you never dreamed of! Look to Me when you're feeling puny, and I'll give you My strength. I'll increase My power in you—even when you're exhausted and overwhelmed, even when you've tried and failed before. Don't give up. Call on Me. Put your hand out in prayer and take hold of My power. Walk with Me and talk to Me and watch for the changes! I'll build spiritual muscle in you to overcome every weakness.

Your Coach and Trainer,
>God

== == ==    == == == == == == == == ==

# THERE'S NOTHING BETTER

**Because your love is better than life,
my lips will glorify you.**

Psalm          63:3

---------------------------------------------

My Dear Child,

>Life is an amazing thing! Your mind thinks and reasons. Your body uses the food you eat to keep you alive. Your skin feels the breeze on your face. Your eyes see the colors of flowers and paintings. The fact that you even exist is an amazing gift. What if you had never been born? You'd never have gotten to experience this wonderful thing called life.

Now let Me tell you a secret: My love is better than life. Think of your favorite song. My love sounds better. Picture the best-looking person in the world. My love looks better. My love is more fun than the most exciting vacation. It's more delicious than the tastiest meal. My love is the source of all good things in life. Ask Me to show you My love and prepare for a super life.

Your Life,
>God

== == ==    == == == == == == == == ==

# STICK WITH JESUS

**Jesus said to them, ". . . You are those who have stood by me in my trials."**

Luke 22:25,28 --------------------

------------------------

Dear Child,

>The disciples found out that being a friend of Jesus wasn't always easy. Sometimes, it meant hard work. Sometimes, it meant people didn't understand or agree with what the disciples stood for. Sometimes, they were excluded by others—even their friends and families.

They were willing to walk the road Jesus walked, even though the road was narrow. They were willing to reach for the standards He set, even though they were high. They were willing to trust the promises He gave them, even though they seemed far off. They were willing to stick with Him through thick and thin, because they knew His love was deeper and wider than anything they had ever known. So stick with Him. He loves you with that same kind of love.

Jesus' Father,
>God

== == ==    == == == == == == == == ==

# I HAVE STAYING POWER

**His dominion is an everlasting dominion, and His kingdom endures from generation to generation.**

**Daniel**        4:34 NASB

---------------------------------------------

My Child,

>The world you live in is here today and will be gone tomorrow. Elected officials hold power only from one election to the next. Investors make a bundle when the market is up and lose it all when the market falls. Popular movie stars watch their popularity evaporate when someone cooler comes on the scene. Musicians at the top of the charts come crashing down when musical trends change.

But I've been on top since the beginning, and I'm not going anywhere. My kingdom has the kind of staying power you'll never find anywhere else. And when you entrust your life to Me, that staying power is yours. I give you a steady strength—a lasting power—an indestructible joy that no one can steal from you.

Your Everlasting Lord,
>God

== == ==    == == == == == == == == ==

# YOUR SAFE ROOM AND SHADE TREE

**He who dwells in the shelter of the Most High will abide in the shadow of the Almighty. I will say to the Lord, "My refuge and my fortress, my God, in whom I trust!"**

**Psalm** 91:1-2 NASB

-------------------------------------------

Dear Child,

>If a tornado were swirling across the land, heading straight for your hometown, you'd probably find some safe, secure room to hide in until the deadly winds had passed. If you found yourself in a desert in the middle of a blinding heat wave, you'd probably be thankful to find a shade tree to sit under.

I want you to understand this about Me: I am your strong, secure room in the rough winds of life. I am your shade tree in the blistering heat of your most difficult day. I am your refuge, your shelter, and your safe place—no matter what's going on. I am a blanket of safety and a covering of confidence. I am the One you can trust. Open your eyes to My reality and your heart to My love. I am here for you.

Your Mighty Fortress,
>God

== == ==    == == == == == == == == ==

# WHO'S YOUR FAVORITE STAR?

**You shall not make for yourself an idol in the form of anything in heaven above or on the earth beneath or in the waters below. You shall not bow down to them or worship them; for I, the Lord your God, am a jealous God.**

**Deuteronomy     5:8-9**

-------------------------------------------

My Child,

>Have you ever been in a restaurant and seen a statue of Buddha? That is an idol: a man-made image that people worship. You've seen other idols, too. Do any of your friends worship rock stars or athletes? There's nothing wrong with respecting or admiring another person, but to cover your room with posters of someone and constantly talk about that person—to be willing to do anything for that person—that's taking things a bit too far.

Is there anything in your life that you think of as an idol? Is there any person, activity, or object that you've placed above Me? Think about it. If you worship your car or your computer, what can mere objects do for you? I am alive, and I want to be involved in your life. Worship Me alone.

Your Creator,
>God

== == ==     == == == == == == == == ==

# MY FORGIVENESS IS RADICAL

**I, even I, am he who blots out your transgressions, for my own sake, and remembers your sins no more.**

Isaiah                43:25

---------------------------------------------

Dear Child,

>Let Me show you how radical My forgiveness is. First of all, when you tell Me about the junk in your life and turn away from it, I immediately forgive you. That's step one. The next thing I do is blot out your sin. I take a big old sponge and soak up the stain of whatever you've done. It's like having a big blob of spaghetti sauce on your white tennis shoes, and the next minute, you can't find a trace of the stain.

But wait, there's more! Not only do I blot up the stain, but once it's gone, I can't even remember that it was ever there! I develop amnesia about it. So please confess your junk and turn the other way. Then I'll do My part. I'll blot it out and forget it!

Your Forgiving Father,
>God

== == ==    == == == == == == == == ==

# DON'T BE AFRAID OF LIFE

When I am afraid, I will put my trust in You. In God,
whose word I praise, in God I have put my trust;
I shall not be afraid. What can mere man do to me?

**Psalm      56:3-4 NASB**

---------------------------------------

Dear Child,

>I realize there's a lot out there to be afraid of—school violence,
drive-by shootings, and abuse. Every day the headlines blare out
another reason for living in fear. It's enough to make you want to pull
the covers over your head and stay there.

But when you feel afraid, I want you to stop and put your trust in Me.
Picture your trust as a small wooden box. When you feel afraid, I
want you to see yourself taking that wooden box and deliberately
giving it to Me. And while you're at it, notice how firmly I take hold of
your trust and keep it safe in My big hands. Don't be afraid. I'm bigger
than anything you fear. I want you to go out there and live your life to
the fullest. Make a difference. And remember that I'm with you today
and every day.

The Trustworthy One,
>God

== == ==    == == == == == == == == ==

# ANALYZE THIS

**God hath not given us the spirit of fear; but of power, and of love, and of a sound mind.**

**2 Timothy**       **1:7** KJV

------------------------------------------

Dear Child,

>Who is this Holy Spirit whom I give to My children? Suppose you could take Him into a laboratory and scientifically analyze Him. What would you find?

First of all, you would find that He contains power—power enough to keep you going even when the going gets tough, power enough to help you fight evil even when it's most deceptive, power enough to overcome any obstacle. You'd also find a sound, balanced, and sensitive but sensible reasoning ability. Most of all, you'd find love— love that isn't proud or envious or impatient, love that protects and trusts and never fails. But try as you might, you could never, ever find fear in My Holy Spirit. I will never give you a spirit of fear.

The Giver of Love and Power and a Sound Mind,
>God

== == ==    == == == == == == == == ==

# FOCUS ON ME

**You have heard that it was said, "Do not commit adultery."
But I tell you that anyone who looks at a woman lustfully
has already committed adultery with her in his heart.**

Matthew        5:27-28

-------------------------------------------

Dear Child,

>Pornography is everywhere now, and it breaks My heart. If you've never seen pornography, that's awesome. Don't ever look at it. If you've already seen pornography, I still love you. You probably feel ashamed because of what you've seen. Maybe you feel like I could never love you again. Here's the solution—tell Me that you're sorry for looking at it, and then stop looking at it. I will wash you clean and remove your guilt.

Does this mean you can't ever look at an attractive person? Not at all. There's a difference between appreciating another person's looks and drooling over them. I think you know the difference. Drooling is lust, and lust will eat your lunch. Give yourself over to lustful thoughts, and you'll feel like a tiny ship tossed around in a hurricane. I don't want your emotions to be out of control like that. Keep your eyes and your heart on Me. I am your anchor.

Your Love,
>God

== == ==    == == == == == == == == ==

# I'LL MAKE A WAY

**I will lead the blind by ways they have not known, along unfamiliar paths I will guide them; I will turn the darkness into light before them and make the rough places smooth. These are the things I will do; I will not forsake them.**

**Isaiah          42:16**

---

Dear Child,

>Do you ever feel like you're caught in a game of blindman's bluff, stumbling blindfolded through life, never quite sure whether you're getting ready to run into a brick wall or step off of a high cliff? I don't want you to feel alone in the dark. I'm right here with you.

When you have to make a hard decision and you're in the dark about what to do, I'll shine My light on the situation so the answer will be clear. When you see everyone else headed down a dark, dead-end alley, stop! Don't go there! I'll be the light that leads you in the right direction. When you feel unpopular for taking a stand and the going gets rough, I'll show up to smooth the path under your feet. Trust Me. I'll make a way for you.

The Pathfinder,
>God

== == ==     == == == == == == == == ==

# IS THAT THE TRUTH?

**You shall not give false testimony against your neighbor.**

**Deuteronomy          5:20**

-------------------------------------------

Dear Child,

>A bully hits a so-called geek on the playground, and everybody sees it happen. The teacher asks, "Did anybody see who hit Elmore?" Nobody says anything. Guess what? All those people just lied, even though they didn't say anything. Anything other than the truth is a lie.

I want you to know the truth. I also want you to speak the truth. Sometimes speaking the truth will make other people mad. But in order to follow Me, you're going to have to stand up and speak the truth. I want you to be so honest that people come to you for your opinion, because they know you'll tell it like it is. If you learn to love the truth, then I will let you speak for Me, because I know I can trust you.

The Truth,
>God

== == ==    == == == == == == == == ==

# JESUS IS THE DOOR TO ME

**I am the door; if anyone enters through Me, he will be saved, and will go in and out and find pasture.**

**John      10:9** NASB

------------------------------------------

Dear Child,

>There is a door that leads directly to My heart. It's not hidden or hard to find. I have made sure that it's right out in plain sight so nobody can miss it. What is this door I'm talking about? My Son, Jesus, is the door that leads to Me, and He's wide open for you to come through. He's closer than your heartbeat—always just a prayer away.

Faith in Jesus is the path that leads through the door into My love, mercy, strength, and the answers you need. So pray in the name of Jesus. Look for the will of Jesus. Put everything in the hands of Jesus, and you'll find yourself inside My pasture where the flock of My family gets fed. What are you waiting for? Come in and chow down!

Your Father,
>God

== == ==   == == == == == == == == ==

# IT'S JUST STUFF

**You shall not steal.**

**Deuteronomy        5:19**

----------------------------------------------

Dear Child,

>Living the Christian life is pretty simple. If you ever wonder what's right, My Bible tells you. And one of the things My Bible tells you is, "Don't steal." If someone works hard to earn something, and then you just waltz in and take it, how can that be right?

It doesn't matter if you think that they won't miss it or that it won't hurt them. It doesn't matter how poor you are or how rich they are. It doesn't matter if they've stolen something from you. Don't steal. If someone else studies hard and you copy their answers, that's stealing, too. Other people's stuff belongs to them—plain and simple. I want you to care more about respecting others and yourself than you do about possessions. Care about people, not things.

Your Guide,
>God

== == ==    == == == == == == == == ==

# TURN ON THE FAUCET

**I will make rivers flow on barren heights, and springs within the valleys. I will turn the desert into pools of water, and the parched ground into springs.**

**Isaiah          41:18**

-------------------------------------------

My Child,

>Maybe your heart is feeling like a desert today—parched and lifeless. You used to laugh and dream and hope, but not now. Right now, you're stuck in this desert, feeling too depressed to change things on your own. Let Me remind you that you're not on your own. I'm here, and I hear every one of your unspoken prayers.

And here's more good news. Piping living water into dry hearts is one of the things I do best! I can come into a desert heart and cause rivers to flow and springs to bubble up. I can create pools in parched places. You hold in your hands the two faucets that turn on My living water: one is trust and the other is praise. When you trust that I can change things and you praise Me for My mercy, before long, the water begins flowing again!

Your Irrigation Specialist,
>God

== == ==    == == == == == == == == ==

# I'M STRONG TO THE FINISH

I love you, O Lord, my strength.

Psalm 18:1

---------------------------------------------

My Dear Child,

>Where would Popeye have been without his spinach? He'd have been toast. Brutus was ten times bigger than Popeye. But as long as Popeye could reach his spinach, Brutus didn't stand a chance.

I'm your spinach. I'm your strength. I guarantee that there are things in life that you aren't strong enough to handle. Don't beat yourself up about it. Come to Me and pray for strength. I can make your mind strong. I can even give your body supernatural strength to keep going. I can make your heart strong when it feels like breaking. I can make your will strong when you feel like giving up. When you're feeling weak, simply pray, "Help me, God." It's not cheating to rely on Me. I want to help you.

Your Strength,
>God

== == ==    == == == == == == == == ==

# TAKE MY WAY AND TRUST MY NAME

They said, "Come, let us build for ourselves a city, and
a tower whose top will reach into heaven, and let us
make for ourselves a name; otherwise we will be
scattered abroad over the face of the whole earth."

Genesis       11:4 NASB

---

Dear Child,

>Since Adam and Eve first decided to taste the forbidden fruit, people have been trying to be gods in their own lives. For instance, long ago, people tried to build a tower that would reach into Heaven. People are still trying to create new ways to Heaven—inventing little self-made religions. But these religions don't lead to Heaven.

Long ago, people also said, "Let us make for ourselves a name." They turned their backs on My name and tried to put their own names up in lights. People are still trying to polish their names and put them in lights. But in the end, their names will tarnish and their lights will go out. Only My way can lead a person to eternal life. Only My name and the name of My Son will last forever.

The Way and the Name,
>God

== == ==    == == == == == == == == ==

# DON'T LOOK BACK!

**Forget the former things; do not dwell on the past. See, I am doing a new thing! Now it springs up; do you not perceive it?**

Isaiah        43:18-19

---------------------------------------------

Dear Child,

>Sometimes it's tempting to look back at your past. Maybe when you do, you see a great time when everything was going your way. That probably causes you to long for those "good old days." Or maybe you see hardships, a broken heart, and dreams that didn't come true. Those things make you feel sorry for yourself or tempt you to dwell on what might have been. Either way, looking back is no way to live.

I want you to find joy in this moment—to look forward to the exciting challenges that lie ahead. I want you to release your yesterdays and reach out to receive My mercies that are new every morning. Don't stay logjammed in the past. I am doing something new . . . right now . . . this minute. Don't miss a single miracle!

The Father of New Beginnings,
>God

== == ==    == == == == == == == == ==

# WAS I TRYING TO IMPRESS YOU?

I will put in the desert the cedar and the acacia, the myrtle and
the olive. I will set pines in the wasteland, the fir and the cypress
together, so that people may see and know, may consider
and understand, that the hand of the Lord has done this,
that the Holy One of Israel has created it.

Isaiah          41:19-20

------------------------------------------

Dear Child,

>I had so much fun designing this world. Like the set designer for a
movie, I dressed the stage, creating deserts, waterfalls, fields, and
mountains. Like a landscaper, I planted trees and vines and flowering
bushes. Like an artist layering color on a canvas, I created glorious
sunsets and seascapes and seasons. Like a master musician, I called
forth a fabulous symphony of sounds—the call of the whippoorwill, the
song of the porpoise, the melody of the meadowlark, and the roar of
the mountain lion.

Why did I go to so much trouble? Was I trying to impress you? You
bet! I wanted you to sit up and be amazed, to know and worship the
One whose hand has made such marvels.

Your Artist and Designer,
>God

== == ==    == == == == == == == == ==

# TO LOVE IS TO OBEY

**The world must learn that I love the Father and that
I do exactly what my Father has commanded me.**

**John          14:31**

-------------------------------------------

Dear Child,

>My Son, Jesus, perfectly obeyed Me. If I told Him to pray for twelve hours, He did. If I told Him not to eat or drink for forty days, He didn't. Why did He obey Me? Because He loved Me. Until you love Me, obeying Me seems like a great big pain. But when you love Me, you'll want to do what I command.

How do you learn to love Me? Start by receiving My love for you. Once you realize how much I love you, that I sacrificed My Son just to be with you, that I have wonderful plans for your life, and that I am proud of you, you'll want to love Me back. Once you love Me, obeying Me won't be a painful duty; it will be a joy.

Your Loving Father,
>God

== == ==    == == == == == == == == ==

# YOU WERE DESIGNED TO TRUST

As for me, I trust in You, O Lord, I say,
"You are my God." My times are in Your hand.

**Psalm**     31:14-15 NASB

--------------------------------------------

My Child,

>Everything is designed to operate by certain principles. Automobiles operate by the principles of internal combustion. Airplanes operate by the principles of aerodynamics. You are a human being, the most complex creation in the world. You were designed to operate by the spiritual principle of trust. You were not designed to carry the weight of the world on your shoulders.

Worry robs you of the peace in which I designed you to live. Worry will only make you sick. So turn your fears and worries over to Me, and I will show you My solutions. You can't control one second of time or how fast a plant grows or how soon springtime will come. But you can learn to trust the One who controls it all.

The Trustworthy One,
>God

== == ==    == == == == == == == == ==

# LOVE ME ON PURPOSE

**Be very careful to love the LORD your God.**

**Joshua        23:11**

---------------------------------------------

Dear Child,

>Some things require great care. You wouldn't juggle knives while daydreaming about the show you saw on TV last night. You wouldn't disarm a bomb and casually read a magazine at the same time. Important things require focus and attention.

I am important. As you seek to follow Me, be attentive. Don't just accidentally stumble through your week hoping you'll eventually get around to spending time with Me. Make an appointment with Me. Mark it on your calendar. Set your alarm. When you come to Me in prayer, turn off the TV. Go somewhere without distractions. Be still and listen. I promise that even in the midst of chaos, you will be more at peace.

Your Focus,
>God

== == ==    == == == == == == == == ==

# HERE'S THE SECRET

**God is love.**

**1 John     4:8**

-------------------------------------------

Dear Child,

>I want to share with you the secret of having a relationship with Me. Once you catch on to this secret, you'll never doubt Me again. I am love. That's the key. Love is the basic ingredient of My character and personality. It's the thought running through My mind, 24/7. It is the breath in My lungs and the beat of My heart. It's the course I am set on, and I will never turn back.

Love is woven so deeply into the fiber of who I am that you can come to Me any hour of any day and know who you'll find: a God of love. My commandments speak with the accent of love. My feet walk the road of love. My Son opens His arms of love, saying, "Come to Me!"

Your Loving Father,
>God

== == ==    == == == == == == == == ==

# I WAS THERE ALL ALONG

**As for me, the nearness of God is my good; I have made the Lord God my refuge, that I may tell of all Your works.**

**Psalm        73:28** NASB

---------------------------------------------

Dear Child,

>Sometimes you feel like I'm right beside you, and other times you feel like I'm far away. When I seem far away, remember this: It's only an illusion. I'm still right here with you. I'm in it for the long haul. In fact, there is no place you can go that's too far away for Me to see or reach you.

So why do you feel like you've lost Me when you haven't? Because sometimes you turn your back on Me. Then you lose sight of Me and feel all alone. Or you put something between us—some worry or fear or some other love that looms so large in your eyes that you lose sight of Me. Put your worries down. Put your other loves below your love for Me, and you'll suddenly see, I was there all along!

Your Forever Friend,
>God

== == ==    == == == == == == == == ==

# THIS IS NOT SCIENCE FICTION

**Behold, I am the Lord, the God of all flesh;
is anything too difficult for Me?**

Jeremiah    32:27 NASB

-------------------------------------------

My Child,

>Lots of people love science-fiction movies. In some of those movies, superhuman beings have imagined abilities that are designed to astound the audience—like amazing strength or speed or intelligence. Human minds created those imaginary beings, but I created human minds. Doesn't that make Me more amazing than the most amazing sci-fi superhero?

There is nothing too difficult for Me—no height too high for Me to reach and no depth too deep for me to plumb. There is no person too lost to be found, if only they'll call on Me. So why would someone as powerful as I am want a friend like you? Because I made you for our friendship. I get a tremendous kick out of you. You make Me so happy!

Your Friend and Superhero,
>God

== == ==   == == == == == == == == ==

# OUR KINGDOM IS DIFFERENT

**The greatest among you should be like the youngest, and the one who rules like the one who serves.**

**Luke        22:26**

-------------------------------------------

Dear Child,

>You probably know some big shots in your school who look down on kids whom they think are not as cool or athletic or popular. Jesus told His disciples in no uncertain terms that they were not to throw their weight around like that, trying to act important. What He told them is exactly what He is telling you today. His kingdom operates on a different scale.

The coolest in My eyes is the one who is not trying to act cool. The one who is willing to take the last place in line is really the one who's in first place. The one who is willing to make friends with that unpopular kid is popular with Jesus and Me. Think about it. Jesus was My Son, yet He came to earth to serve other people. I want you to be like Him.

Your Father,
>God

== == ==    == == == == == == == == ==

# JUST LIKE HEAVEN

**Surely goodness and love will follow me all the days of my life, and I will dwell in the house of the LORD forever.**

**Psalm          23:6**

---------------------------------------------

Dear Child,

>What do you think Heaven looks like? Do you imagine fluffy clouds and fat, flying babies playing harps? That's weird! Let Me paint another picture of Heaven for you. Picture your dream house. Maybe it's a big cabin tucked away in the mountains, overlooking miles of rolling wilderness. Maybe it's a big, glass-fronted beach house overlooking a clear blue bay and miles of remote sandy beaches. Imagine the most cozy house you can.

Now imagine all your friends and favorite people are there. There's lots of great food. The music is wonderful. You are having the time of your life. And the reason all of this is possible is because I'm the host. Heaven is a place that I've made for you. If you've asked My Son, Jesus, to be in charge of your life, your place in Heaven is reserved. Living in My house forever will be Heaven.

Your Heavenly Host,
>God

== == ==    == == == == == == == == ==

# TURN ON YOUR HEADLIGHTS

**Your word is a lamp to my feet and a light for my path.**

**Psalm          119:105**

-------------------------------------------

Dear Child,

>Have you ever tried to find your way down a path in the dark without a flashlight? You can't make a whole lot of progress, can you? You stumble over every bump in the road. You can't even be sure if you're headed in the right direction. For all you know, you could be going around in circles.

Trying to make it through life without the light of My Word is like that. It's like asking to get lost—like signing up for a lifetime of bumps and detours and wrong turns. But reading My Word is like turning on your headlights. Suddenly, you are able to see clearly! And even though you can't see where the road ends, you'll be able to see where you are and how to get there. So pick up My Word and turn on the lights.

The Headlights of Your Life,
>God

== == ==    == == == == == == == == ==

# DON'T FORGET WHO STARTED IT ALL

**Who has measured the waters in the hollow of his hand, or with the breadth of his hand marked off the heavens? Who has held the dust of the earth in a basket, or weighed the mountains on the scales and the hills in a balance?**

Isaiah          40:12

--------------------------------------------

My Child,

>I take pride in much of the progress people have made. I see the beautiful skyscrapers, the highways, and bridges. I see the medical discoveries that bring healing to people who suffer. I see the amazing advancements in the fields of technology and communication.

But I also see the proud hearts of people. They forget that none of these achievements would have been possible had I not created a world of natural resources. None of this could have been done apart from My gifts of human intelligence and reason. People make gods out of money or progress or their own abilities, forgetting to turn to the One who was here from the beginning and brought the whole earth into being. Don't be like those who forget. Remember Me.

Your Creator,
>God

== == ==    == == == == == == == == ==

# LET MY WORDS BE WRITTEN ON YOUR LIFE

Jesus answered and said to him, "If anyone loves Me,
he will keep My word; and my Father will love him,
and We will come to him and make Our abode with him."

John        14:23 NASB

-------------------------------------------

Dear Child,

>Suppose you had a friend who told you twenty times a day how
much he liked you. But then the first chance he got, he hurt your
feelings or stole your money or started a rumor about you. How good
a friend would he be? A friend is someone who is loyal—someone who
chooses to act in ways that prove his words of friendship are true.

I want you to show your friendship for Me with more than words. I
want your life to be so full of My love that people won't have to
wonder whether you're My friend. They'll just look at you and see My
words and My ways written all over your life and they'll know. Then
My Son and I will come and set up housekeeping in your heart and
live with you day and night.

The One Who Befriends You,
>God

== == ==    == == == == == == == == ==

# MY NAME MEANS "PROVIDER"

**Abraham called that place The Lord Will Provide. And to this day it is said, "On the mountain of the Lord it will be provided."**

**Genesis        22:14**

---------------------------------------------

Dear Child,

>One of My most powerful names is "Jehovah-Jireh" which means "Provider." It means that I am the God who provides for My children. A long time ago, Abraham learned a lesson about My provision—a lesson he never forgot. Abraham was willing to sacrifice his son, but I provided a ram instead. Abraham learned that although I sometimes test, I also provide.

That's true for you, too. Whatever the circumstances or the situation—in trials, in temptation, in tests—keep your eyes open for My provision, and you'll find it there. Look for Me in the midst of your hardest times, and you'll find Me there, providing whatever you need—wisdom, strength, hope, and faith.

Your Provider,
>God

== == ==    == == == == == == == == ==

# GROW UP!

**Grow in the grace and knowledge of
our Lord and Savior Jesus Christ.**

2 Peter             3:18

--------------------------------------------

Dear Child,

>You can grow in so many different ways. You can grow to be taller,
fatter, more obnoxious, or more educated. You can grow in social
maturity or worldly sophistication. You can grow more cynical or silly,
more independent or self-satisfied.

But I am asking you to grow in two all-important ways. Grow in the
grace and in the knowledge of your Lord and Savior Jesus Christ.
This is the growth that really changes you. To grow in His grace is to
become a person of compassion, just like Jesus. To grow in your
knowledge of Him is to provide good ground in which your faith can
flourish. So grow up in the things of the Spirit—in His grace and the
knowledge of Him.

The Source of Grace and Knowledge,
>God

== == ==    == == == == == == == == ==

# LET OTHER PEOPLE KNOW

**We have heard with our ears, O God; our fathers have told us what you did in their days, in days long ago.**

Psalm 44:1

---

Dear Child,

>Once you get to know Me, one of the best things you can do is to tell other people how I'm working in your life. Maybe you used to feel depressed, but since you've started to trust Me and read My Word, you have begun to feel hopeful instead. Maybe you used to feel like an outsider, but since you've started to trust Me, you're part of a new group—a group that's excited about what I'm doing. Those are your own personal miracles.

I know that parting the Red Sea was a miracle. But believe Me, parting a sea of depression is awesome, too! I know that creating a world was pretty good. But creating a new group of friends is amazing, too. So tell others about Me. Gossip about the Good News. They need to know Me just like you do.

The Source of Everyday Miracles,
>God

== == ==    == == == == == == == == ==

# A CHEERING CROWD

**Since we have such a huge crowd of men of faith watching us
from the grandstands, let us strip off anything that slows us down
or holds us back, and especially those sins that wrap themselves
so tightly around our feet and trip us up; and let us run with
patience the particular race that God has set before us.**

**Hebrews         12:1** TLB

------------------------------------------

Dear Child,

>Do you realize that up in Heaven, all the great men and women of
faith are cheering for you—Moses and Abraham, Ruth and Sarah,
Peter and Paul, and Jesus Himself? All of them are looking down
from their heavenly grandstand as you run your own race of faith. All
of them are shouting, "Go for it! Don't stop! You can do it!"

What is your race? I have asked you to live out your faith in the
middle of your world—right where you are—in your family, in your
school, on your street. I have asked you to untangle yourself from the
temptations that try to trip you up so that you can step out in love,
reach out in mercy, and take My words of hope to people in despair.
So get in the race and trust Me. You're not running alone. I'm right
here beside you!

Your Coach,
>God

== == ==    == == == == == == == == ==

# I'M ON THE LOOKOUT!

**The eyes of the Lᴏʀᴅ range throughout the earth to strengthen those whose hearts are fully committed to him.**

2 Chronicles          16:9

---------------------------------------------

Dear Child,

>I'm on the lookout for somebody special. I'm on twenty-four-hour alert looking for a certain person I want to bless and strengthen. Who is this mysterious person you may ask? Actually there's nothing mysterious about it.

I'm looking for anyone whose heart is sold out to Me—anyone whose mind wants to think My thoughts, anyone who's trying with every bit of spiritual energy to follow in My footsteps. When I find a person like that, there's nothing I won't do to give that person all the energy that's needed to make and keep a commitment to Me! You don't have to live a perfect life to please me. It's enough to find a heart that longs for a relationship with Me.

The One Who Searches,
>God

== == ==    == == == == == == == == ==

# I'M YOUR FATHER

**Faithful is He who calls you,
and He also will bring it to pass.**

1 Thessalonians        5:24 NASB

---------------------------------------------

Dear Child,

>When your teacher gives you an assignment, she expects you to do the work yourself. If there is research to do, she expects you to go to the library and look up the information. If there is writing, she expects you to put your own ideas on paper with all the proper spelling and punctuation. She's not going to follow you around saying, "I know you can do it. Go, kid, go!" And she certainly won't go to the library and do the work for you.

Well, I'm not like your teacher. I'm your Father. And the assignments I give you matter more than any term paper. That's why I will never give you an assignment without giving you the power to do the work. I'll even be doing the work in you and through you. I'm 100 percent in your corner!

Your Faithful Father,
>God

== == ==     == == == == == == == == ==

# I WANT YOU TO KNOW ME

**The people who know their God will
display strength and take action.**

**Daniel        11:32** NASB

-------------------------------------------

Dear Child,

>I want you to know Me so well that any doubts you've ever had
about Me will totally evaporate. I want you to have a deep, true,
childlike faith in Me that nothing can shake. That kind of faith can only
be yours when you get in touch with who I really am and what I'm
really like—when you begin to understand that I am on your side, that
I can't wait to take up for you when others are against you, and that I
love you with a love that has no limits.

Knowing all these things, you'll be surprised at your boldness and
ability to take action in situations that once would have intimidated
you. Your boldness will spring not from your own strength, but from
the knowledge that My strength is shielding and sheltering and
covering you all the time. The key to boldness is knowing Me.

Your Friend and Father,
>God

== == ==    == == == == == == == == ==

# BREAK THE ICE

**We love because he first loved us.**

**1 John          4:19**

-------------------------------------------

Dear Child,

>Have you ever gotten into an argument with a friend that went something like this?

"You're being mean to me."
"Well, you started it."
"Well, I wouldn't have started it, if you weren't being so mean."
"Well, I would be nice now, but you're still being mean."

How does an argument like that get settled? Eventually, someone has to take the first step to be nice. Then the other person will soften up. My Son, Jesus, took the first step with you. When you were mad at Me, when you didn't believe in Me, when you were being mean to Me and to other people, Jesus broke the ice and said, "I'm going to love you anyway." Since Jesus loves you, you can be the one to love others first. You can be the one to break the ice. You don't need everybody else to love you first, because Jesus already did.

Jesus' Proud Father,
>God

== == ==    == == == == == == == == ==

# LET MY STRENGTH SHOW UP IN YOU

**He said, ". . . I am with you; that is all you need.
My power shows up best in weak people."
Now I am glad to boast about how weak I am; I am
glad to be a living demonstration of Christ's power,
instead of showing off my own power and abilities.**

**2 Corinthians     12:9 TLB**

---------------------------------------------

Dear Child,

>There is no place in the world that My power shows up better than in people who are willing to admit they need help. The minute I hear one of My kids saying, "God, help me! I can't handle this," is the minute My power kicks into overdrive.

When a huge, muscular guy with an I.Q. of 200 does something amazing, everybody just says, "What did you expect?" Nobody's surprised. Even if I had helped him, nobody would believe it. They'd just chalk up his accomplishments to his own strength and intelligence. But if a person who's been weak in the past is suddenly strong, and he's willing to say, "It was God! God did it in me!" everybody will sit up and take notice. Some of them will turn to Me and believe. Thank Me for your weaknesses.

Your Strength,
>God

== == ==    == == == == == == == == ==

# I CAN QUENCH YOUR THIRST

**They drink their fill of the abundance of Your house;
and You give them to drink of the river of
Your delights. For with You is the fountain of life.**

**Psalm**     **36:8-9** NASB

\-\-\-\-\-\-\-\-\-\-\-\-\-\-\-\-\-\-\-\-\-\-\-\-\-\-\-\-\-\-\-\-\-\-\-\-\-\-\-\-\-\-\-\-\-\-

My Child,

>Look around you. You see people caught in every kind of addiction:
alcohol, drugs, food, sex, and gambling. And the list goes on. Why
have so many people put their lives in such dangerous places? They
have a crazy, outrageous thirst that they can't seem to quench, and
most of them don't even know what it is.

They don't realize that they are thirsty for Me—for My presence, My
companionship, My words, and My love. So they just keep taking
these big poisonous gulps of the wrong stuff, while their souls keep
dying of thirst. I want you to know that I have an abundance of the
only water that will satisfy you. It is living water. Lead the thirsty ones
to Me.

The Fountain of Life,
>God

== == ==    == == == == == == == == ==

# PITY AND PRAY FOR THEM

**Many are saying about me, "God won't rescue him." But, Lord, you are my shield, my wonderful God who gives me courage.**

**Psalm        3:2-3 NCU**

-------------------------------------------

Dear Child,

>You might have some friends who think you're pretty much of a weirdo and a loser for believing in Me. They might even laugh in your face or talk about you behind your back because you're putting all your trust in someone who's invisible.

Well, if that happens to be the case, I want you to pity and pray for them. Pity them because they don't have a friendship with the One who loves with an everlasting love. And pray that their blind eyes will be opened so they can see beyond this little box of physical reality into the huge sphere of spiritual vastness. Also know this, I will not let their cynical remarks turn you away from Me. I'll be your shield and your closest friend.

The One Who Hands Out Courage,
>God

== == ==    == == == == == == == == ==

# MY LOVE SURROUNDS YOU

**You are all around me—in front and in back—and have put your hand on me. . . . Where can I go to get away from your Spirit? Where can I run from you? . . . If I rise with the sun in the east and settle in the west beyond the sea, even there you would guide me. With your right hand you would hold me.**

**Psalm 139:  5,7,9-10 NCV**

-------------------------------------------

Dear Child,

>Have you ever seen a little baby playing peekaboo with her daddy? When she holds her blanket up over her face, she thinks he can't see her anymore. She hasn't learned yet that her daddy's love is a whole lot bigger than that blanket! It surrounds and sees her from all sides. It won't let her out of his sight.

That's the way My love is for you. I am in front of you and in back of you. I'm above you, watching over you, and below you, holding you up. You might have times when you want to run away and hide from Me. Maybe you already have. But here's what I want you to understand: My eyes see you wherever you are, My heart loves you no matter what you're going through, and My hand is reaching out to welcome you home.

Your Daddy,
>God

== == ==    == == == == == == == == ==

# WORK IS A FACT OF LIFE

**Tackle every task that comes along, and
if you fear God you can expect his blessing.**

**Ecclesiastes          7:18** TLB

-------------------------------------------

Dear Child,

>Everyone has to work. That's just a fact of life. It's your attitude that makes an enormous difference in whether you enjoy your work and do it well, or you grumble and slack off. A slacker may not work as hard, but that doesn't make life any easier. It only breeds dissatisfaction.

When enthusiastic, energetic people pitch in to help, they will finish up feeling great about themselves and the work. So before you begin a job—whether it's raking the yard or writing a paper—pray first. Remember that I'm here with you and I care. Work hard and enjoy yourself, knowing that I'll be working right alongside you.

Your Loving Father,
>God

== == ==    == == == == == == == == ==

# YOUR BODY IS A MIRACLE!

**I plead with you to give your bodies to God. Let them be a living sacrifice, holy—the kind he can accept. When you think of what he has done for you, is this too much to ask?**

**Romans          12:1** TLB

---------------------------------------------

Dear Child,

>Your body is a miracle, a treasure, and a gift. I designed it, and I'm proud of My work! Consider what an amazing thing it is that without even giving it a thought, you can take exactly the right amount of oxygen into your lungs every time you breathe! Your heart is pumping at exactly the right rate per minute, delivering blood through a complex set of vessels and veins that wind like tiny highways throughout your body. Your digestive system is processing and distributing the food you swallow.

Only I could make you as you are. Only I can keep you running. Only I know the true and important purposes for which you were designed. Think about all I've done for you and give back to Me what I've given to you—yourself. Is that too much to ask?

Your Designer and Mechanic,
>God

== == ==    == == == == == == == == ==

# DO WHAT PILOTS DO

**What is faith? It is the confident assurance that something we want is going to happen. It is the certainty that what we hope for is waiting for us, even though we cannot see it up ahead.**

**Hebrews     11:1 TLB**

----------------------------------------

Dear Child,

>An airline pilot probably wouldn't get into the cockpit unless there was someone in the tower to help the aircraft arrive safely at its destination. Should bad weather set in, the pilot knows someone in the tower can radio advice on how to proceed through a blinding fog or rain. Should an oncoming aircraft get off track and start heading toward the plane, the pilot may not see it, but the air-traffic controller will pick it up on radar and advise the pilot about what to do. That's why the pilot's faith is in the tower.

If you put your trust in Me, I can guide you through the rough weather of life. That's why I'm asking you to put your faith in Me.

Your Strong Tower,
>God

== == ==   == == == == == == == == ==

# ACTIONS SPEAK LOUDER THAN WORDS

**You yourselves are our letter, written on
our hearts, known and read by everybody.**

2 Corinthians          3:2

-------------------------------------------

Dear Child,

>Are you more impressed by someone who makes a rousing speech
about world hunger or by someone who gives away money to feed a
hungry family? Are you more impressed by someone who writes a
newspaper article about ending racial discrimination or by someone
who makes a true friend with someone of a different racial or ethnic
background? Don't actions always speak louder than words? They do
to Me.

There are people all around you who may never read the Bible. But
they will read the letter of your life, and hopefully they'll say, "There's
just something about that person that's different. What is it? I want it!"
So write My words on your heart where they can make a difference in
your world.

The Author of Your Life,
>God

== == ==    == == == == == == == == ==

# WILL YOU GO?

**In you the fatherless find compassion.**

**Hosea          14:3**

-------------------------------------------

My Child,

>In the streets of Calcutta, India, right now, a twelve-year-old girl begs for food. She has no parents. She is sick and malnourished. She has been sexually abused so many times it seems normal to her. She is just one of literally millions of parentless street children in the cities of the world. Where will she find compassion?

Why am I telling you this? Because there are hurting people all around. Seek Me as to your role—how you are to get involved, and with whom and where. Perhaps I want to bless you financially to help send missionaries to the field. Perhaps you want to get involved in a more direct way. Certainly you can pray. Let's spend some time together so that I can share My will for your life. Whatever your role is in My work, I promise it will be more fun than you ever dreamed. And as in all giving, you will receive back far more than you are capable of giving.

The Father of All,
>God

== == ==    == == == == == == == == ==

# THIS IS NOT A NORMAL WAR

**Our fight is not against any physical enemy: it is against organisations and powers that are spiritual. We are up against the unseen power that controls this dark world, and spiritual agents from the very headquarters of evil.**

**Ephesians    6:12 PHILLIPS**

--------------------------------------------

Dear Child,

>Do you ever put your head on the pillow at night feeling whipped—almost like you've been in a battle? That shouldn't surprise you too much, because you have. But it's not a normal war with normal weapons. It's a spiritual war. The weapons are invisible, spiritual weapons and your enemy is invisible, too. He uses words to persuade you to give up. He uses thoughts to tell you you're no good.

Maybe you're saying, "Hold it! Don't get spooky on me. I'm not buying that devil, demon, darkness bit." But I'm saying, "I want you to take Me seriously and use My weapons to fight this war." My weapons are the Word of truth, the gospel of peace, prayer, and faith in My Son. Finally, it's important to remember this as you go out each day: The battle is Mine, and the victory's already been won! Trust Me.

Your Captain,
>God

== == ==    == == == == == == == == ==

# YOU'RE NO PAPER DOLL

**Do not conform any longer to the pattern of this world, but be transformed by the renewing of your mind. Then you will be able to test and approve what God's will is—his good, pleasing and perfect will.**

**Romans          12:2**

-------------------------------------------

Dear Child,

>Some people in this world would like to see you fit like a paper doll in a string of other paper dolls. They would encourage you to clone your thoughts from the tame, safe, unoriginal thoughts of others. If they had their way, your clothes, friends, hobbies, and all your activities would be as much like everybody else's as possible. Maybe you know people who live their lives like that—desperate to fit in with the world's idea of what's important. Maybe you've even tried it yourself.

Well, enough is enough. It's time to stop conforming to the world and start letting Me transform your life and renew your mind. I want to light your life up with original, God-inspired ideas so that you can know My will and step out into the radically exciting future I've got mapped out for you.

The One Who Transforms,
>God

== == ==    == == == == == == == == ==

# TUNE IN TO MY PROGRAM

**Make sure that you don't get so absorbed and exhausted in taking care of all your day-by-day obligations that you lose track of the time and doze off, oblivious to God. The night is about over, dawn is about to break. Be up and awake to what God is doing!**

**Romans 13:** 11-12 THE MESSAGE

------------------------------------------

Dear Child,

>I realize your life can be exhausting at times. Some days you must feel like you're living in a room full of TV sets, computer programs, and video games all running at once. I know it's tempting to try to concentrate on everything at once. But if you do, your mind can easily become overloaded.

Of all the conflicting screens in that room you call your life, there is only one that contains total, life-changing, now-and-forever truth. That's the screen that contains My program. It's the screen that reveals My heart trying to make contact with yours. So don't get so confused and distracted with other programs that you miss out on Me and Mine. Wake up. Tune in. Log on.

Your Webmaster,
>www.God.heaven

== == ==    == == == == == == == == ==

# SPEND TIME WITH THE ONE WHO IS PEACE

**May the Lord of peace himself give you peace at all times and in every way.**

2 Thessalonians 3:16

-------------------------------------------

Dear Child,

>If you were in the market for great sports equipment, you'd probably look for somebody who knew a lot about sports and sports equipment and was selling it at a reasonable price. Am I right?

Well, if you'd like to have more peace in your life—if you'd like to be less stressed, calmer, and more confident—there is someone I want to put you in touch with. His name is Jesus. He's My Son, and He knows everything there is to know about peace and calmness and confidence. He's not only the Lord of peace, He is peace. Deciding to make friends with Jesus and spend time with Him is deciding to get rid of a lot of the stress in your life.

As you talk to Jesus and listen to Him, He'll bring more peace into your life than you thought possible. Spend time with the One who *is* peace.

Jesus' Father,
>God

== == ==    == == == == == == == == ==

# KEEP ON GOING!

**By your endurance you will gain your lives.**

Luke          21:19 NASB

-------------------------------------------

Dear Child,

>In the 1992 Olympic Games, in the backstretch of the 400-meter race, a British runner named Derek Redmond fell flat on his face. What a heartbreak! In that moment, he knew that all his years of training and his dream of winning the gold medal were lost.

So what did Derek do? Did he sit down and cry? Did he kick and scream and try to blame the other runners? No. As painful as it was, Derek struggled to his feet and began hopping down the track on his one good foot! Derek's dad, Jim Redmond, came bounding out of the stands and put his arms around his son. One step at a time, he helped his son over the finish line.

Derek Redmond acted as I want you to act. He didn't quit. He kept on. Your race won't be an easy one, but I'll be with you through it all.

Your Supporter,
>God

== == ==    == == == == == == == == ==

# CLOSE THE GAP

**Now that you know these things,
you will be blessed if you do them.**

John     13:17

-------------------------------------------

Dear Child,

>There is a huge gap between knowing something and doing it. Just because you have a map of San Francisco doesn't mean you've been there. Just because you've got a recipe for your Great-Aunt Mamie's chicken potpie doesn't mean it'll be on the table for dinner tonight. Just because you know the dimensions of a basketball court and watch it on TV doesn't make you a basketball player.

What really counts is the person who is willing to step out and act on what he or she knows about Me and My kingdom. Jesus was all action. He didn't just show up on earth one day saying one thing and doing another. Instead, He came to demonstrate what My kind of person is like. I want you to do what Jesus did. Close the gap between what you know and what you do.

The Lord of Action,
>God

== == ==    == == == == == == == == ==

# FIND YOUR PLACE

**Show proper respect to everyone: Love the brotherhood of believers, fear God, honor the king.**

1 Peter          2:17

--------------------------------------------

My Child,

>When you were born into this world, you were immediately born with certain titles. You were born a baby, but you were also born a citizen, a neighbor, and even a tax deduction. As you grew up, you assumed more titles—student, teen, member, and friend.

You may be surprised to know that one of your most important titles is simply "human being." As a person, you owe every other person respect, because all people are made in My image. Another important title you have is "citizen." As a citizen, you owe police officers, teachers, and even trash collectors respect, because they work to help you. And you owe the leaders of your country respect, regardless of whether they are good or bad. (Be sure to pray for them.) Finally, as My child, you owe Me respect. I want you to live up to your titles. Be an example to others of how a person should act.

Your King,
>God

== == ==    == == == == == == == == ==

# LOOK WHO'S COMING

As he approached the town gate, a dead person was
being carried out—the only son of his mother, and
she was a widow. . . . When the Lord saw her,
his heart went out to her and he said, "Don't cry."

Luke        7:12-13

---

My Child,

>Can you imagine this scene? A big funeral procession is coming
down one side of the street, carrying the coffin of a dead boy.
Everybody is wearing black and crying. Meanwhile, down the other
side of the street, here comes Jesus and his friends, laughing, talking,
and joking around. Suddenly, these two groups bump into each other.

Does Jesus say, "Oh, I'm so sorry! Excuse me. We should be crying,
too"? No, He tells the mother of the dead child, "Don't cry." Don't Cry!
Her only son had just died. Who is this stranger saying, "Don't cry"?
But then Jesus gives her a reason not to cry. Right there in the street,
He brings her son back to life! Suddenly, everybody is partying, not
just Jesus and His friends, but all the mourners, too. My Son has a
way of turning bad to good in a split second. Are you sad right now?
Don't cry. Here comes Jesus!

Jesus' Father,
>God

== == ==    == == == == == == == == ==

# YOU CAN MAKE A DIFFERENCE

**Watch your step. Use your head. Make the most of every chance you get. These are desperate times!**

**Ephesians 5:** 15-16 THE MESSAGE

-------------------------------------------

Dear Child,

>I could have mapped out a life for you with no hard choices and no dead ends. I could have locked you into life like a plane on automatic pilot and delivered you from the day of your birth to Heaven's front door with no possible pitfalls.

But instead, I have given you a life with lots of options, choices, and chances. And what's more, I have set you down in the midst of a generation that is difficult and desperate. Kids your age are faced with more life-threatening problems and temptations than ever before. So why did I put so much responsibility in your hands? I believe you can handle it. I believe that with My Son beside you and My Spirit within you, you can make a difference in your world. So trust Me! Step out! Make the most of every opportunity.

The One Who Believes in You,
>God

== == ==    == == == == == == == == ==

# LET ME REDECORATE

**You deserve honesty from the heart; yes, utter sincerity and truthfulness. Oh, give me this wisdom.**

**Psalm        51:6** TLB

---------------------------------------

Dear Child,

>I created you with a private room in your life—a room called your heart—and nobody but you holds the key. Your friends can't get into that private heart-room unless they're invited. Your parents can't either, and though I'm the great God of everything, even I'm not powerful enough to kick the door down and get in unless you want Me there. Oh, I can look in through the windows and see what's hidden inside, but only you can ask Me in.

If I had permission, I would come in and redecorate. I'd strip the gray of hypocrisy from the walls and paint them in the clear, bright colors of sincerity. I'd lay down beautiful woven carpets of honesty, and furnish your heart with graceful, comfortable furniture of wisdom. So turn the key and ask Me in. Then wait till you see your new heart!

Your Decorator,
>God

== == ==    == == == == == == == == ==

# LOUE 'EM ALL

**I will heal their waywardness and love them freely,
for my anger has turned away from them.**

**Hosea        14:4**

----------------------------------------

My Child,

>Do you know people who hate Me, who don't believe in Me, or who make fun of My children and My Church? How do you feel about those people? Do they make you mad? Do they make you want to argue? Do you want to tell them, "God's not like that"?

How do you think I feel about the people who hate Me, who don't believe in Me, or who laugh at Me? I love them. Does that surprise you? I love them even though they are confused and wounded. A badly wounded dog growls at everybody, even the vet who tries to help. Don't let those growling dogs scare you away. They desperately need love. Do you love Me? Then love them for Me. They may change their minds about Me. I can heal and save them.

The Lord of All,
>God

== == ==    == == == == == == == == ==

# IT GETS BETTER

**Weeping may remain for a night, but rejoicing comes in the morning.**

**Psalm         30:5**

-------------------------------------------

My Child,

>If anybody tells you, "Christians don't have any problems. It's all just cake and ice cream!" that person is either lying or confused. Sometimes sadness comes into your life. It can even bring you closer to Me. So the next time you're sad, ask Me to help.

Come to Me and let Me comfort you. I still love you. And I won't let you stay sad forever. Life is full of ups and downs, but the most important thing is for you to stay close to Me. If something bad happens to you, it doesn't mean I've stopped loving you. I will never stop loving you. Don't be afraid. I am with you, even in sadness.

Your Comforter,
>God

== == ==    == == == == == == == == ==

# COME IN FOR A HEART TRANSPLANT!

A new heart also will I give you, and a new spirit will I put
within you: and I will take away the stony heart out of your
flesh, and I will give you an heart of flesh. And I will put my
spirit within you, and cause you to walk in my statutes,
and ye shall keep my judgments, and do them.

Ezekiel 36:26-27 KJV

------------------------------------------

Dear Child,

>One of the great breakthroughs in medical science occurred when doctors learned to perform heart transplants. They discovered a procedure for removing old, diseased hearts that could barely keep patients alive and exchanging them for new, healthy hearts that would give patients a new chance at life.

My heart transplants are spiritual. I never give My patients a new heart without including a new spirit in the deal. Here's how I operate. I reach into the life of any person who calls on Me and exchange a stony, sinful heart for a heart like Mine—one that beats with My love and compassion. I also give that person a new spirit and My Holy Spirit. With My Spirit in your life, you actually have the power to live like I live. What an operation!

Your Heart Specialist,
>God

== == ==    == == == == == == == == ==

## I'VE BEEN CALLING YOU

I took you from the ends of the earth, from its farthest
corners I called you. I said, "You are my servant";
I have chosen you and have not rejected you.

Isaiah        41:9

------------------------------------------

Dear Child,

>Maybe you remember the day you first called My name. Maybe you
were in some kind of jam, and you decided it was time to send an
S.O.S. to Heaven. Well, that's not really how it happened. You weren't
the first to call. I've been calling you since I first created you. All
along, I have wanted you to become one of My kids—a member of
My family.

You may not realize it, but you are only reading this book right now
because somewhere in your heart, you heard a still, small voice
urging you to reach out for Me. Over all the competing sounds of CD
players and TV shows, I've been calling. Close to your heart, I've
been whispering, "I love you. I have chosen you. Will you give your
life to Me?" Now that you've heard Me, what's your answer?

The Still, Small Voice,
>God

== == ==    == == == == == == == == ==

# DON'T GET STUCK IN YOUR FEAR

Some men came and told Jehoshaphat, "A great multitude is coming against you from Edom. . . ." Then Jehoshaphat feared, and set himself to seek the LORD.

**2 Chronicles    20:2-3 RSV**

------------------------------------------

Dear Child,

>What can you learn from a king who lived thousands of years ago? A lot! Jehoshaphat, the king of ancient Judah, understood something I want you to understand. Here's the scene: A messenger rushed into Jehoshaphat's courts shouting the news that the powerful army of Edom was on its way to attack Judah. At first, Jehoshaphat had a natural reaction. He freaked out! But it only took him a minute to settle down and look to Me. Jehoshaphat knew where to get help, and he didn't waste time.

So what's My point? It's okay to feel afraid. Everybody's scared from time to time. But don't stay scared. Pray right away. I'm waiting here to help you whenever you need Me.

The One Who's on Your Side,
>God

# JUST KEEP READING

**The unfolding of your words gives light;
it gives understanding to the simple.**

**Psalm          119:130**

-------------------------------------------

Dear Child,

>Not everyone can be a rocket scientist. Not everyone can be a philosopher. Not everyone can be a great inventor. But everyone can read the Bible. As you read the Bible, it unfolds itself just like a note. When you open a note that your friend has passed to you, first you see a corner of the note, then you see half of the note, and finally you see the whole thing.

If you don't understand everything in the Bible right away, that's okay. Learn from the things you do understand and just keep reading. Gradually, the Bible will unfold itself. A light will switch on in your head. You'll say, "Oh, I get it," and your life will never be the same in that area. You may not be a rocket scientist, but you can be wise. Just keep reading My Book.

Your Wisdom,
>God

== == ==    == == == == == == == == ==

# TRUST THE ARTIST

**How terrible it will be for those who argue with the
God who made them. They are like a piece of broken
pottery among many pieces. The clay does not ask
the potter, "What are you doing?" The thing that is
made doesn't say to its maker, "You have no hands."**

Isaiah             45:9 NCV

--------------------------------------------

Dear Child,

>How would you like it if you were creating a beautiful painting, and it
jumped down off the easel and began whining at you for using red
instead of purple? How would you like it if you were turning an
exquisite bowl on the potter's wheel, and it began fussing at you for
making it one way instead of another? I know that sounds silly.
Paintings and pottery don't talk back. But bear with Me. I'm making a
point here.

You see, I'm in the process of creating you. I know exactly what I'm
doing. When you grumble and gripe about your height, your coloring,
your musical talent, or athletic ability, you are insulting Me, your
maker. I'm making you for My purposes. I know exactly how I want to
use you. And it's going to be good. Trust Me!

The Artist of Your Life,
>God

== == ==    == == == == == == == == ==

# THE WORDS SHOW THE HEART

**Good people have good things in their hearts,
and so they say good things. But evil people
have evil in their hearts, so they say evil things.**

Matthew        12:35 NCV

------------------------------------------

Dear Child,

>Did you ever play the game Clue? In it, you try to solve a mystery by putting together a series of clues. Just like the game, you can learn how to solve the mystery of what's in a person's heart by paying attention to certain clues. For instance, listen to the words that come out of a person's mouth. That's a pretty good clue to what's inside.

People who gripe, gossip, and put other people down all the time have a lot of garbage in their hearts. People who find good things in bad situations, who are thankful and funny and love to encourage others, have good things in their hearts. You're not going to find prickly pears growing on apple trees or avocados growing on grapevines. The fruit that grows on a tree tells you what kind of tree it is.

Your words are the fruit of your life. Let Me give you My words.

The Gardener,
>God

== == ==    == == == == == == == == ==

# MEMBERSHIP HAS ITS PRIVILEGES

**How great is the love the Father has lavished on us, that we should be called children of God! And that is what we are!**

**1 John          3:1**

----------------------------------------

Dear Child,

>The best title that anyone could have is "child of God." Being a child of God means that the Creator of everything is your Father. Since I am the King of the universe, that makes My children royalty. My children have My favor, protection, and love.

If you are My child, it means you carry My name. I trust you to do things for Me that no one else gets to do. You get to tell people about Me. You get to go on special missions to bring My love into dark places.

But mostly, being My child means you can talk to Me anytime you want, and I'll listen. I'm not a Father who is gone all the time. My main job is raising you. You may become famous, you may even become the president, but your most important title will still be "child of God."

Your Father,
>God

== == ==    == == == == == == == == ==

# STICK TO WHAT YOU KNOW

**God is our refuge and strength, an ever-present help in trouble. Therefore we will not fear, though the earth give way and the mountains fall into the heart of the sea, though its waters roar and foam and the mountains quake with their surging.**

**Psalm          46:1-3**

---------------------------------------------

Dear Child,

>There have always been people in every age who have spread the rumor that the sky is falling or that the end of the world is coming next Thursday. When Jesus was asked to pinpoint the end of time, He made it clear that no one would know when it was coming.

So why should you get all bogged down in what you don't know? I'd much rather see you stick to what you do know—that I am your refuge and your strength, your source of help when trouble comes. Fear can't trap you when you're sure of Me. Let the mountains fall! Let the ocean rage! Let the hills shake, rattle, and roll! I'm bigger than they are, and I'm in charge of protecting you. So tune out the fear pushers and hear this: I'm your Dad and I can handle it!

Your Refuge,
>God

== == ==    == == == == == == == == ==

# STARTING OVER

**If anyone is in Christ, he is a new creature; the old things passed away; behold, new things have come.**

**2 Corinthians**     **5:17** NASB

---------------------------------------------

Dear Child,

>Have you ever felt like you had blown it so badly that you couldn't start over? No way! No matter how badly you think you've messed up, there is always a starting-over place. That place is a personal relationship with Me through My Son.

When you establish a relationship with Jesus, He gives you a whole new beginning. His forgiveness helps you to look back at the old things almost like they happened to someone else. He gives you hope to look forward to new things with the faith and innocence of a little child. The best thing about this new relationship with My Son is that He gives you His Spirit to help you live with the same courage and compassion that He did. Are you ready?

The Lord of New Beginnings,
>God

== == ==  == == == == == == == == ==

# THESE RULES ROCK!

**Your statutes are wonderful; therefore I obey them.**

**Psalm            119:129**

---------------------------------------------

My Child,

>Are all rules equal? If someone were to make up a silly rule you had to follow to join a group, which rule would you like better—eat ice cream after every meal or stand on your head in the corner for an hour every day? Unless you're allergic to ice cream, you'd probably like the first rule better. That may seem farfetched, but the world is full of rules that are just as absurd.

One rule says that women have to walk five feet behind their husbands. Another rule says that people have to face a certain direction when they pray. Those aren't My rules, so don't even worry about obeying them.

My rules are all good. Obeying them will make a major difference in your life. My most important rule is to love God (Me). My second best rule is to love other people. If you obey these rules, your life will be wonderful. And don't worry, I'll help you keep them.

Your Teacher,
>God

== == ==    == == == == == == == == ==

# SOMETIMES IT'S GOOD TO HATE

**Hate evil, love good.**

**Amos          5:15**

---------------------------------------------

Dear Child,

>Is it okay for Christians to hate? Well, it says in the Bible to hate evil. There are certain things you should hate. Hate the devil. Hate injustice. Hate evil. It's never right to hate people, but it's right to hate the evil they do. In other words, don't hate Hitler—hate the evil he did.

Of course, hating evil is only half of the picture. I also want you to love good. Love it when someone does the right thing. Love it when someone is nice to a kid everyone calls a geek. Love it when someone paints a beautiful picture or sings a beautiful song. If you love good, you'll begin to do good. If you hate evil, you'll begin to overcome evil with good. I hate evil. I love good. Be like Me.

The Giver of All Good Things,
>God

== == ==    == == == == == == == == ==

# YOU CAN WALK ON WATER, TOO

**"Come," he said. Then Peter got down out of the boat, walked on the water and came toward Jesus.**

**Matthew        14:29**

---

Dear Child,

>One day Jesus wanted to spend some time alone praying, so He sent His friends ahead of Him in a boat to cross the Sea of Galilee. When it got dark, the wind started howling and the sea got rough. Suddenly, they saw Jesus walking toward them on the water. All of them were majorly spooked, thinking He was a ghost! So He called out, "Don't worry, guys. It's just Me." That's when Peter said, "If it's You, let me come to You." So Jesus said, "Come on," and Peter found out how it feels to walk on water. The only time he started to sink was when he took his eyes off of Jesus and looked at the storm.

Here's the lesson for you. Don't get focused on the rough winds of your circumstances. Keep your eyes on Jesus, and He'll hold you up!

His Father and Yours,
>God

== == ==    == == == == == == == == ==

# SURPRISE!

**You also must be ready, because the Son of Man will come at an hour when you do not expect him.**

**Luke          12:40**

-------------------------------------------

Dear Child,

>Has anybody ever given you a surprise birthday party? You walked into your house expecting to make a peanut-butter sandwich and do a little homework, and all of a sudden there are lights, balloons, decorations, birthday cake, and all your best friends laughing and shouting, "Surprise!"

Well, guess what. When Jesus comes back, it'll also be like a surprise party. Jesus will know where and when, but you won't have a clue. Jesus always shows up in unexpected places and ways. (Take the manger, the cross, and the empty tomb, for instance.) That's why you need to be ready for His return. Any day of the week could be the one. And I definitely want you at the party!

Your Host,
>God

== == ==    == == == == == == == == ==

# SMALL FAITH EQUALS BIG RESULTS

**Who despises the day of small things?**

**Zechariah          4:10**

-------------------------------------------

Dear Child,

>It's easy to look at powerful people in the Bible and say, "I could never be a Moses or a David or a Mary." Let Me tell you something that might surprise you. Each of them had only one thing going for them in the beginning—faith.

Moses told Me he couldn't speak well enough to confront Pharaoh for Me. I said, "Trust Me, Moses." He did, and he set My people free. David was just a kid with a slingshot who went out against a raging giant. But David believed I was with him, and he brought Goliath down. Mary was just a teenage girl, but because she believed the words of an angel, she became the mother of Jesus.

My mightiest accomplishments began on a day of small beginnings. My most powerful people are those who give Me faith the size of a mustard seed.

The One Who Works with Small Things,
>God

== == ==     == == == == == == == == ==

# KEEP IN STEP WITH ME

**Enoch walked with God.**

**Genesis          5:24**

\-\-\-\-\-\-\-\-\-\-\-\-\-\-\-\-\-\-\-\-\-\-\-\-\-\-\-\-\-\-\-\-\-\-\-\-\-\-\-\-\-\-\-\-\-\-

Dear Child,

>If I could wish one thing for your life, what would it be? That you would know Me. Not just know about Me, but really know Me.

Enoch was like that. He knew Me. He walked with Me. What do I mean by that? Enoch learned to keep in step with Me. He knew Me so well that he could tell when I was ready to speed up and move into action, and he could tell when I was planning to lie back and chill out for a while. He gauged the speed of his footsteps by the speed of Mine. He knew all the ins and outs of the roads I traveled. It was not a religious, Sunday school kind of knowing. It was an everyday knowledge of My presence that he experienced in the ordinary moments of his life.

I want you to walk with Me like Enoch did. Are you ready?

Your Friend,
>God

== == ==    == == == == == == == == ==

# COME LIVE IN MY LOVE

**Make yourselves at home in my love.
If you keep my commands, you'll remain intimately
at home in my love. That's what I've done—kept my
Father's commands and made myself at home in his love.**

**John 15:9-10**     THE MESSAGE

----------------------------------------------

Dear Child,

>My love for you is like the home you've always dreamed about and
longed for. Every room is furnished with great stuff—thick rugs,
comfortable chairs, and a view from every window. When you walk in
the front door, you almost have to stop and stare. There's something
so familiar. It's like you've been here before and you're finally home to
stay! The reason you get this feeling is that you were created to live
in My love full time, enjoying My friendship forever.

How can you pull that off? By living the way I designed you to live.
Jesus lived like that. He lived full time within the boundaries of My
perfect commands for His life. That's why He was able to live full time
within the walls of My perfect love. You can, too.

Your Architect, Builder, and Host,
>God

== == ==    == == == == == == == == ==

# GIVE IT YOUR BEST

**Always give yourselves fully to the work of the Lord, because you know that your labor in the Lord is not in vain.**

1 Corinthians        15:58

-------------------------------------------

My Child,

>When you do something for Me, I want you to go all out. If I tell you to visit a nursing home and listen to the older people there, don't just sit there rolling your eyes while they talk and leave in five minutes. Pay attention, smile, and get into it. I have told you to obey your father, so don't just say, "Yeah, Dad, whatever." Say, "Yes sir," and then quickly do what he told you to do.

If you are a Christian, people are watching to see how you work. They want to see whether there's anything different about you. Will you complain like so many other people when it comes to work? Will you cut corners and do a halfhearted job? Work hard and do your best. You are a reflection of Me.

Your Boss and Your Father,
>God

== == ==    == == == == == == == == ==

# GUARD THE SPRING OF YOUR HEART

**Watch over your heart with all diligence,
for from it flow the springs of life.**

**Proverbs 4:23**     NASB

---------------------------------------------

Dear Child,

>Let Me tell you a story. Once there was a child who drank every day from a bubbling spring. Because the spring water was pure, the child grew to be healthy and strong. Then one day while she was off playing, her enemy came and put a few drops of poison in the spring. That's all it took. Not knowing of the poison, the child continued to drink the water daily, and gradually, she began to feel sick and sad.

Now let Me explain. The spring is your heart where your thoughts and emotions live. Satan is your enemy who wants to poison your heart with his lies. But when you trust Me, I'll pour My truth into your heart, washing away Satan's lies. And I'll help you build a wall around the spring to guard your heart.

Your Gatekeeper,
>God

== == ==    == == == == == == == == ==

# HAVE I GOT A PLAN FOR YOU!

**It is God himself who has made us what we are and given us new lives from Christ Jesus; and long ages ago he planned that we should spend these lives in helping others.**

Ephesians     2:10 TLB

---------------------------------------------

Dear Child,

>I never just create a person and throw him down in the middle of life and say, "There! Make something of yourself." I have a plan for every life, including yours. You probably didn't look for My plan right away. Most people don't. You might even be in the middle of trying out your own plan right now. Maybe it's not working so well. Maybe you've even fallen flat on your face and discovered what failure feels like. That's okay. Sometimes that's what it takes before a person begins to look for Me.

But know this: Trusting Jesus as your Savior is the first step in discovering My plan for you. That's when you find out how great it feels to do what you were made to do—to use your gifts as you work alongside Me to help others.

The Planner and the Plan,
>God

== == ==    == == == == == == == == ==

# A PICTURE OF JOY

**For you who fear my name, the Sun of Righteousness
will rise with healing in his wings. And you will go free,
leaping with joy like calves let out to pasture.**

Malachi          4:2 TLB

--------------------------------------------

Dear Child,

>Have you ever been on a farm when the calves are being let out of
their pen? If you have, then you've seen a picture of total joy! They
come romping and leaping out into the pasture, kicking up their heels
like a bunch of little kids at recess. That's the kind of joy and freedom
I want you to feel inside. It's the kind of joy and freedom I have in
store for all of My children who know Me and praise My name.

When you taste My forgiveness and try on My new life, the reality of
My presence will rise in your heart like the sun on a dark day, pushing
back the shadows and burning off the fog. Your sadness will be
comforted, and your wounds will be healed. Your fears will be put to
rest, and your weakness will be filled with My strength. Trust Me.

The Father of Joy,
>God

== == ==    == == == == == == == == ==

# A TREASURE AND A GIFT

**Everything God made is good, and we may eat it gladly if we are thankful for it, and if we ask God to bless it, for it is made good by the Word of God and prayer.**

1 Timothy        4:4-5 TLB

---------------------------------------------

Dear Child,

>Early Jewish Christians had to learn how to live in the freedom Jesus came to give. As Jews, they had followed strict Jewish dietary laws, but as followers of Jesus, they had to learn that all food is good if it is eaten thankfully. Maybe you have put yourself under strict dietary laws, too, counting calories and fat grams and feeling guilty if you eat "sinful" foods that aren't on your diet. You may have even developed anorexia or bulimia.

I don't want you to live like that anymore. I love you too much. Your body is a treasure to be honored. Food is a gift to be enjoyed. Let Me set you free from your prison of dietary laws. Let Me teach you to eat thankfully and without fear. This kind of freedom is possible in Me.

The Giver of Life,
>God

== == ==    == == == == == == == == ==

# MIND YOUR STEP

**Great peace have they who love your law,
and nothing can make them stumble.**

**Psalm          119:165**

-------------------------------------------

Dear Child,

>When you go hiking, would you rather wear sturdy hiking boots or slippery church shoes? Not a tough choice. With the boots, you can step anywhere. If you land in water, no problem—boots are waterproof. If you step on a thick root, no problem—boots absorb the shock. But go hiking in slippery church shoes, and you'll spend half your time falling down.

My Word is like hiking boots. Love My Word, obey it, and you'll be prepared to hike through life. You'll never have to worry about whether you're disobeying Me. You'll know what I want, you'll be doing it, and you can step wherever you like. People who hate My Word walk through life, slipping and sliding, never really sure whether they are right or wrong and always wondering if I'm mad at them. I love you either way, but you'll have a more enjoyable journey if you walk in the boots of My Word.

Your Traction,
>God

== == ==    == == == == == == == == ==

# LIKE FATHER, LIKE SON

**While he was still speaking, a bright cloud enveloped
them, and a voice from the cloud said, "This is my Son,
whom I love; with him I am well pleased. Listen to him!"**

Matthew      17:5

---------------------------------------------

My Child,

>Have you ever seen a father and son who look exactly alike, eating
in a restaurant? The son will look just like a younger version of his
father. They sound alike. They have the same facial expressions.
They may even hold their forks the same way.

I want you to know what I'm like, and the best way to know Me is to
know My Son, Jesus. He is just like Me. I sent Him to show you what
I'm like. When He was on earth, He did exactly what I asked Him to
do. He said exactly what I told Him to say. Read His words. You can
find most of them in the Gospels (Matthew, Mark, Luke, and John). If
you'll do what Jesus said (and He said some radical things), then
you'll be doing exactly what I want.

Jesus' Father and Your Father, Too,
>God

== == ==    == == == == == == == == ==

# LET'S TALK

**Pray all the time. Ask God for anything in line with the Holy Spirit's wishes. Plead with him, reminding him of your needs, and keep praying earnestly for all Christians everywhere.**

**Ephesians       6:18** TLB

-------------------------------------------

Dear Child,

>When I tell you to pray all the time, I don't mean you need to stay on your knees all day or walk around constantly mumbling to yourself. You'd look pretty silly, and you'd get fed up with prayer in no time.

Let Me explain what praying all the time means. Your mind is never silent anyway. It's always got thoughts running through it, like *Uh-oh. Looks like rain. And I don't have a ride home from band practice.* Instead, try praying, "Lord, here comes the rain. How am I going to get home?" Then I might say, "Why don't you ask Jessie for a ride?" And if you do, you might end up with a new friend!

Prayer is a simple conversation between you and Me. It's both of us talking and both of us listening.

Your Prayer Partner,
>God

== == ==    == == == == == == == == ==

# LIKE MONEY IN THE BANK

**He will keep in perfect peace all those who trust in him, whose thoughts turn often to the Lord!**

**Isaiah          26:3 TLB**

-------------------------------------------

Dear Child,

>Every time you take your thoughts off of your worries and turn them to Me, you're depositing peace into your spiritual bank. Every time you use your energy for trusting Me instead of wasting it on fretting, you're adding more peace to your spiritual bank account. Your trusting thoughts of Me remind you that I'm in control. No matter what is troubling you, I am more powerful. No matter what is worrying you, My love is greater.

As you continue to deposit your trusting thoughts of Me into your spiritual bank, they will gather interest and grow. Pretty soon, you will have a huge treasure of peace to draw on when stressful situations spring up. So think of Me often and trust in Me. I won't disappoint you.

Your Peace Giver,
>God

== == ==    == == == == == == == == ==

# I DON'T THINK LIKE YOU DO

**How great are his wisdom and knowledge and riches! How impossible it is for us to understand his decisions and his methods! For who among us can know the mind of the Lord? Who knows enough to be his counselor and guide?**

**Romans      11:33–34 TLB**

-------------------------------------------

Dear Child,

>Sometimes you look at what's going on in the world, and you want to say, "God, what are You up to? This doesn't make sense!" When that happens, it shouldn't surprise you. You were not designed to understand everything about Me.

You see, I don't think like you do. In fact, it's actually impossible for you to get inside My mind and understand My God-thoughts. That's why it would be a mistake for you to try to figure out everything and give Me advice. You weren't cut out to be My counselor. The best thing you can do is to know My character—that I am a good and faithful Father who will never let you down.

Trust Me in every situation as I lead you, and you'll find yourself living in more peace than you thought possible.

The Higher One,
>God

== == ==    == == == == == == == == ==

# WORTH WAITING FOR

**Wait for the L**ORD**; Be strong and let your heart take courage; yes, wait for the L**ORD**.**

**Psalm          27:14** NASB

---------------------------------------------

Dear Child,

>You live in a world that wants instant everything. Every morning, people stir up cups of instant coffee. At noon, fast-food restaurants serve lines of drive-through customers (and if the service isn't fast enough, you can see the customers through their car windows impatiently drumming their fingers on the dashboards). There are instant dry cleaners and instant drugstores. It's only a matter of time before people will want drive-through lines at church to receive instant Communion!

But I am not an instant God. I want you to learn patience—to grow strong and courageous as you learn to wait on Me. There is no discipline that builds spiritual muscles like waiting.

The One Worth Waiting For,
>God

== == ==    == == == == == == == == ==

# MAKE YOUR OWN MONEY

**Make it your ambition to lead a quiet life, to mind your own business and to work with your hands, just as we told you, so that your daily life may win the respect of outsiders and so that you will not be dependent on anybody.**

1 Thessalonians      4:11-12

--------------------------------------------

My Child,

>I want you to have the things you need—a home, food, and clothing. I don't want you to have to borrow money from a credit-card company or a bank for everyday necessities. When you borrow from someone, you are dependent on that person. How can you tell someone at the bank, "God loves me, and He provides for my every need," when they know you owe them $3,000?

If you are always borrowing from people, that makes you dependent upon them. I want you to be dependent on Me. Right now, you are somewhat dependent on your parents, and that's fine. But as you grow up, I want to make you financially independent of them. So work hard now and mind your own business. This will help you develop into a mature adult, dependent only upon Me.

Your Provider,
>God

== == ==    == == == == == == == == ==

MORE E-MAIL FROM GOD

# IN THE MARKET FOR CONFIDENCE?

**I am still confident of this: I will see the goodness of the LORD in the land of the living.**

**Psalm          27:13**

------------------------------------------

Dear Child,

>Have you ever noticed that some people just seem to have an air of confidence about them? What makes for real confidence? Is it looks or brains, money or clothes, or maybe popularity? It might surprise you to know that some of the people who look the most confident on the outside are really the most insecure. I know because I can read their thoughts. Inside, they're thinking, *I wonder what she thinks of me?* or, *Does this outfit make me look fat?* or, *What if I say the wrong thing?*

Real confidence comes from knowing Me, knowing that I love you unconditionally, and I'll never, ever let you down. A gut-level understanding of that reality will make you strong, confident, and steady as a rock. Believe Me.

Your Confidence,
>God

== == ==     == == == == == == == == ==

# YOU CAN SEE THE INVISIBLE

**He persevered because he saw him who is invisible.**

**Hebrews        11:27**

------------------------------------------

Dear Child,

>Mountain climbers have to overcome all kinds of obstacles: uncertain and torturous weather conditions, soreness and injuries, oxygen that gets thinner the higher they go, and the extra weight of equipment they have to carry. On every climb, there are numerous temptations to turn back. But committed climbers have learned to endure by focusing on a mental picture of their destination—the mountain's summit.

You also face daily obstacles that tempt you to give up on life, but you can endure as the climbers do by keeping your mind focused on the face of My Son. Picturing His loving face through eyes of faith will give you courage enough to stay on the journey. Jesus is the summit of your spiritual journey. Keep climbing!

The Mountaintop,
>God

== == ==   == == == == == == == == ==

# IT'S NOT RELIGION, IT'S A RELATIONSHIP

**You can never please God without faith, without depending on him. Anyone who wants to come to God must believe that there is a God and that he rewards those who sincerely look for him.**

**Hebrews       11:6 TLB**

-------------------------------------------

Dear Child,

>It may surprise you to know that I'm not the slightest bit interested in religion—the traditions, buildings, and stained-glass windows. That's not what I'm about. What I want is for us to have a relationship—a friendship—where I can talk to you and you can talk to Me at anytime and about anything. You might be thinking that it's pretty hard to talk to somebody you can't even see. I know. But that's where faith comes in.

Faith is believing in what you can't see. Faith is showing up in the early hours of the morning with your Bible in your lap, believing that I'll meet you there. The reward of faith is that when you show up believing I'll be there, I will! Don't miss out on the excitement of the faith adventure that's waiting for you when you learn to trust Me.

The Friend Who's Waiting,
>God

== == ==    == == == == == == == == ==

# YOU CAN TRUST THE GOD SQUAD

**I am going to keep on being glad, for I know
that as you pray for me, and as the Holy Spirit
helps me, this is all going to turn out for my good.**

**Philippians      1:19 TLB**

---------------------------------------------

Dear Child,

>When you're in the middle of a mess, surrounded by trouble, it's
sometimes hard to imagine anything but a terrible outcome. That's
where faith comes in. Believing in Me means trusting that a powerful
team is at work full time on your problem, no matter how impossible
it looks.

My Son, the Holy Spirit, and I are on call 24/7. We never rest. We love
you and know what's best for you. You can also get a couple of close
Christian friends to pray for you. Then you'll have a total God squad on
your side. Do you believe that? If you do, you've got all the faith you
need, and you can be glad, no matter what you're going through. It's
going to work out for your good and My glory. I'm here to help.

Your Problem Solver,
>God

== == ==    == == == == == == == == ==

# GET WISE

**Those who have insight among the people
will give understanding to the many.**

**Daniel        11:33** NASB

----------------------------------------

Dear Child,

>The more you hang out with Me, the wiser you become. My wisdom
points out solutions to problems and helps you make good choices.
It's like you've been walking around in a fog, and when you start
following Me, the fog lifts, and you see clearly.

Why do I give you wisdom, insight, and understanding? To help you
take the right road? Sure! That's one of the reasons. But it's more
than that. When I make one of My kids wise, I also do it so they can
help others who are still walking around in a fog. How do you help?
Not by being pushy or acting like a big know-it-all. But by being a
friend and praying for others and allowing Me to show you quiet ways
to share your faith. Trust Me. I will guide you.

The Wisdom Giver,
>God

== == ==    == == == == == == == == ==

# SECRET FOR SUCCESS

**In everything you do, put God first, and he will direct you and crown your efforts with success.**

**Proverbs**     **3:6** TLB

-------------------------------------------

Dear Child,

>Want to know a secret for success that works for every profession, from the business person to the ballerina, or the taxi driver to the tax attorney? It also works for students! What's the secret? Put Me first.

Putting Me first works for every person because I made every person. I gave each of you gifts and abilities. I suited each one of you for a certain work, and when you turn to Me, I can guide you to success. Sometimes I'll do that by showing you how to work more efficiently or study harder. Sometimes I'll do it by teaching you to get along with a certain teacher or coach or boss you might not like. Sometimes putting Me first will simply unlock for you the freedom of trusting or the joy of learning. Put Me first. You'll see.

Your Secret for Success,
>God

== == ==   == == == == == == == == ==

# PRAYER IS NOT A PERFORMANCE

**When you pray, go into your room, close the door and pray to your Father, who is unseen. Then your Father, who sees what is done in secret, will reward you.**

Matthew          6:6

-------------------------------------------

Dear Child,

>Have you ever noticed how some people show off when everybody's watching? Some people even show off at church, praying loud and long, just so everyone will see how spiritual they are. But then I don't hear from them for the rest of the week.

If you want to pray to Me, don't be a show-off about it. I don't want your prayer to be a fancy speech performed in front of a crowd. Just get off by yourself where nobody can hear and start talking to Me. If you really want to talk to Me, you don't need an audience. It's okay to pray with other people, too, but if that's the only kind of praying you ever do, what kind of a relationship do we have?

Your Unseen Father,
>God

== == ==    == == == == == == == == ==

# I'LL SHELTER YOU

**He will shield you with his wings! They will shelter you.**

**Psalm** **91:4** TLB

------------------------------------------

Dear Child,

>Ever get caught in a thunderstorm with rain pelting your face and body and lightning striking all around? Pretty frightening! Or maybe you've been in really severe weather, like a hurricane or a tornado. Did you know that I hear from more people during weather like that than at almost any other time?

I love for My children to call out to Me. I love to answer your S.O.S. prayers, because that's one way I can prove to you I'm real. When you're in trouble and you call to Me and I answer, that adds muscle to your faith! So let Me shelter you from all kinds of things, not only bad weather, but from hurt feelings, broken relationships, and tough circumstances. I'll shelter you and shield you with My wings.

Your Protector,
>God

== == ==    == == == == == == == == ==

# BE REAL WITH ME

**Will the Lord reject forever? Will he never show his favor again? Has his unfailing love vanished forever? Has his promise failed for all time? Has God forgotten to be merciful? Has he in anger withheld his compassion?**

**Psalm          77:7-9**

-------------------------------------------

Precious Child,

>When you feel abandoned by Me, I am still here. Sometimes you will go through hard stuff, but as I help you overcome, you'll get stronger. Sometimes you feel down, depressed, or really confused. But I am always here. Think of it this way: Sometimes the speedometer on a car breaks. The car is still going, but the speedometer reads zero.

Maybe that's the way it is with us right now. You know I'm here, but you can't feel Me. Try banging on the dashboard. Seriously, cry out to Me. It's okay to say how you feel. If you feel lost, say, "God, where are You?" If you feel confused, say, "God, I don't understand." I just want you to be real with Me. I am here. I will hear you, and I will answer. Hang in there.

Your Deliverer,
>God

== == ==    == == == == == == == == ==

# WHAT COMES AROUND GOES AROUND

**Blessed are the merciful, for
they will be shown mercy.**

**Matthew          5:7**

------------------------------------------

Dear Child,

>Sometimes in English class, your teacher will have you read your
paper out loud, and afterwards, everybody gets to comment on it. You
might really enjoy making fun of someone else's paper, but the
meaner you are to them, the meaner they will be to you when your
turn comes.

There's a lesson to be learned in that. If you cut people slack when
they mess up, they will most likely cut you slack when you mess up. If
you demand perfection from everyone, they will demand perfection
from you. Here's an extra twist: If you cut people slack when they
mess up, I will cut you slack when you mess up. But if you expect
everyone to be perfect, I will expect you to be perfect, too. I want to
be merciful to you, so help Me out by being merciful to others.

Your Forgiver,
>God

== == ==    == == == == == == == == ==

# GET RID OF THE MONSTERS

**The LORD is my light and my salvation; whom shall I fear?**

**Psalm       27:1** NASB

------------------------------------------

Dear Child,

>When you were a little kid, were you ever afraid of the dark? Did monsters seem to lurk in the dark shadows of your room after the lights were off? The world can sometimes feel like that, too, when you are in spiritual darkness.

So here's what I want to do. Let Me come into the rooms of your heart and turn on the light of My love. Let Me shine in every dark corner of your life and chase away all the monsters you've been putting up with. It's time for you to be whole, healed, and totally Mine. It's time for you to let Me help you get rid of anything that's been holding you back or pulling you down—sins, fears, any bad memory from the past, or any dread of the future. I can do it.

The Light,
>God

== == ==    == == == == == == == == ==

# IT'S NOT A SUPERSTITIOUS S.O.S.

The LORD is near to all who call on him, to all who call on him in truth. He fulfills the desires of those who fear him; he hears their cry and saves them.

Psalm        145:18-19

-------------------------------------------

Dear Child,

>I'm never so near to you as when you call on Me in truth. What do I mean by calling on Me in truth? It's when you're looking for Me and praying with faith. It's not when you're just throwing out some kind of superstitious S.O.S., like a message in a bottle or a penny in a well.

I've got the engine running, and I'm ready to speed into action for My kids who truly love and fear Me. Don't misunderstand the word "fear." I don't mean I want you to be shaking in your boots (although if you really knew My size, you might!). I do want you to respect whom you're dealing with. I'm your loving Father and Friend, but I'm also the Ruler of the universe! So call on Me in faith and fear . . . and believe Me, I'll be here.

The Almighty,
>God

== == ==    == == == == == == == == ==

# MAKE PEACE

**Blessed are the peacemakers, for they will be called sons of God.**

Matthew          5:9

-------------------------------------------

My Child,

>Sometimes, when two groups can't agree, they will hire a peacemaker, a person who stands in the middle of the two groups and helps them make peace. The peacemaker talks them through their differences in a calm, logical manner. If the peacemaker is successful, the two groups reach an agreement, the problem is solved, and both sides benefit.

I want you to be like that peacemaker. If you get into an argument with someone, it's okay to express an opinion, but your goal should always be peace. There will always be someone with whom you disagree, but disagreements don't have to lead to anger. Things don't have to get personal. I want you to be fair and sensible, even in an argument. Then you will be like Jesus.

Your Peace,
>God

== == ==    == == == == == == == == ==

# WANT A HAPPY LIFE?

**Happy is the man who doesn't give in and do wrong when he is tempted, for afterwards he will get as his reward the crown of life that God has promised those who love him.**

James          1:12 TLB

-----------------------------------------

Dear Child,

>You might have the idea that the person who gives in to temptations is the one who has all the fun in life. You might look at the guy who's doing drugs or drinking, the girl who's purging to stay thin, the kid who's smarting off to teachers, and the sexually promiscuous person and think they're really happy. But the rebellion you're seeing is a sure sign of unhappiness.

If the rebellious person felt good about life, he or she wouldn't have to prove anything. It's the person who doesn't give in to the temptation to do wrong who is truly happy. Inside, that person feels good, stable, and at peace with Me. Want to feel happy about your life and yourself? Don't give in to temptation. I'm here to help you.

Your Strength,
>God

== == ==    == == == == == == == == ==

# I AM THE RIVER

**There is a river whose streams make glad the city of God, the holy habitation of the Most High. God is in the midst of her, she shall not be moved.**

**Psalm      46:4-5 RSV**

---------------------------------------------

Dear Child,

>The kingdom of God is anywhere My Holy Spirit dwells. That means if you have trusted Me as your God and Jesus as your Savior, then the kingdom of God is in you! And running right down through the main street of your being, there is a river—an amazing, powerful, sparkling river of life. It is a river that makes you strong in a way you'll never be strengthened by taking vitamins or lifting weights or running a triathlon. It's a river that sends spiritual strength throughout your entire personality to fill up your whole being.

So be aware of who you are in Me and who I am in you. Your heart houses My Spirit, and I am the current of life that flows through you. Live in this reality, and nothing will knock you down!

The River,
>God

== == ==    == == == == == == == == ==

# HOLD ON TO ME

**In all these things we overwhelmingly conquer through Him who loved us.**

**Romans 8:37 NASB**

---------------------------------------------

Dear Child,

>During World War II, a Dutch watchmaker named Corrie ten Boom was imprisoned in the Nazi death camps for helping Jews escape from Holland. There she endured the loss of beloved family members—her father and her sister, Betsie. She was beaten and starved. She was exposed to terrible weather, wearing little clothing, and was cruelly humiliated by the guards. And yet she could echo Paul's words with all her heart: "In all these things we overwhelmingly conquer through Him who loved us."

You probably haven't had an opportunity to test the truth of those words to this degree yet. But I want you to know this. No matter what you go through in your life, if you hold on to Me, you'll find out that those words are true. In My love, you can conquer all things.

Your Ever-Present Father,
>God

== == ==    == == == == == == == == ==

# YOU'VE GOT SOMETHING THEY NEED

**The conquering power that brings
the world to its knees is our faith.**

1 John 5:4    THE MESSAGE

---------------------------------------------

Dear Child,

>When you look at others, I know it's easy to feel small by comparison. Maybe the popular kids who win school elections impress you or maybe it's the brain who aces every test without even studying. Or maybe it's the super jock, the class clown, or someone who plays in a band you look up to.

That's okay. Go ahead and admire them, but remember that you've got something they need. If you are living in My presence, trusting Me, you contain enough power to change a life or heal a heart or give someone reason to believe—enough power to conquer anything! That power is faith—faith in Me and My Son. So hold your head up and take your faith to school each day, loving others as Jesus did.

Your Power,
>God

== == ==    == == == == == == == == ==

# STAY PUT

**Remain in my love.**

**John          15:9**

-------------------------------------------

My Wonderful Child,

>To remain means to stay. If you remain in the car, you don't get out and go into the grocery store. If you remain in marriage, you don't get a divorce. I want you to remain in My love. Some people go to church and feel My love, but then the next day they forget about Me and do their own thing. That's not remaining in My love.

You don't have to think, *Remain in God's love. Remain in God's love,* like a robot all day long. But when you do think of Me, just pray silently, *Yes, Lord, I'm still here with You.* If you remain in My love, you won't ever have to wonder, *Does God love me today?* I will always love you every day. I want you to feel so comfortable and at home in Me that it never occurs to you to leave and do your own thing. So remain in My love. It's where you belong.

Your Loving Father,
>God

== == ==     == == == == == == == == ==

# UNWRAP YOUR GIFTS

**Do not throw away your confidence, which has a great reward. For you have need of endurance, so that when you have done the will of God, you may receive what was promised.**

**Hebrews     10:35-36** NASB

--------------------------------------------

Dear Child,

>You are like a little kid on Christmas morning who has barely begun to unwrap his gifts. One of the most precious gifts under the tree is still wrapped. It's the gift of confidence. It's a gift that is valuable not only for itself, but because it comes with an added bonus. Just like a pizza with a coupon taped to the box that's good for a free order of bread sticks, you can redeem the coupon on your "box" of confidence for the added gift of endurance.

Endurance is the gift of keeping on going even when the going gets tough. And trust Me, keeping on in the Christian life is what leads to the real rewards! So start unwrapping your gifts. And don't throw your confidence out with the wrapping paper! You're going to need it.

The Gift Giver,
>God

== == ==    == == == == == == == == ==

# READ YOUR MAIL

**Whatever was written in earlier times was written
for our instruction, so that through perseverance and
the encouragement of the Scriptures we might have hope.**

**Romans        15:4 NASB**

-------------------------------------------

Dear Child,

>Don't you love to see those three little words on your computer
screen: "You've Got Mail"? If you think an e-mail is special, think
about how special it was to get a letter during Bible times. A letter was
often written with the most primitive of tools and delivered by boat or
on horseback or even on foot.

The Bible is a letter written long ago and sent through time and space
from My heart to yours. My Holy Spirit inspired the writers of each
book to write down My messages to you. Those messages contain
words of instruction to encourage you and help you hold on through
all the junk that comes against you. They contain words of hope that
say, "Don't give up. I love you and I always will." So read your "mail."

The Writer of the Book,
>God

== == ==    == == == == == == == == ==

# HOW TO CHOOSE WELL

**I will go to the king, even though it is against the law. And if I perish, I perish.**

**Esther          4:16**

-------------------------------------------

Dear Child,

>Esther was a beautiful young Jewish woman who became the queen of Persia, but her husband, the king, didn't know she was Jewish. Esther found out that an evil man named Haman was plotting to have all the Jews in the land put to death, and she knew she had to tell the king about the plot. But the penalty for approaching the king without being summoned was death. So here was Esther's dilemma: Should she risk death to save her people or should she save her own neck and let them die? Esther saved her people, and her own life was spared.

Like Esther, you'll have some important choices to make in your life—choices that may be risky. Come to Me when you need the wisdom and courage to choose well.

Your Counselor,
>God

== == ==    == == == == == == == == ==

# INTRO TO WORLDMAKING 101

**Give thanks to the Lord of lords . . .**
**who by his understanding made the heavens.**

Psalm 136:3,5 ------------------

---------------------------

My Child,

>Have you ever written a term paper? Have you ever put together a
bicycle? Have you ever built a rocket? Anyone who is smart enough
to do any of those things deserves respect. That person must be
creative. They must be hardworking. They must know a lot.

Now, have you ever built a world? I didn't think so. I'm the only One in
the whole world who knows how to build the whole world. I not only
created the world, I thought it up. I thought up all the birds in the
world, and then I made them. I thought up the sky and the mountains
and the beaches, and then I made them. Thank Me. Respect Me. No
one knows as much as I do. Can you trust Me to help you with your
math homework? I think so.

The Creator of Everything,
>God

== == ==    == == == == == == == == ==

# WHO DO YOU SEE IN THE MIRROR?

**You shall love your neighbor as yourself.**

**Mark**     12:31 NASB

--------------------------------------------

Dear Child,

>It breaks My heart when you are critical of other people. But it breaks My heart every bit as much when you are critical of yourself, putting yourself down for every tiny mistake and hating the person you see in the mirror. I'm asking you to stop criticizing yourself and start loving yourself.

One reason loving yourself is so important is that you'll never learn to love others until you learn to love yourself. If only you could see yourself through My eyes. In My eyes, you are so awesome, so valuable, so full of potential. If you could ever get a glimpse of yourself as I see you, you'd never be able to put yourself down again. You'd actually start believing in yourself and loving yourself, too. Then you can let that love spill over to others.

The One Who Is Love,
>God

== == ==    == == == == == == == == ==

# THIS PRODUCT NOT SOLD IN STORES

**O Lᴏʀᴅ, God of Israel, there is no God
like you in heaven or on earth.**

**2 Chronicles          6:14**

------------------------------------------

Dear Child,

>Why are Van Gogh's paintings worth so much money? Because
each one is an original. Van Gogh only painted so many, and then he
died. There will never be another Van Gogh painting. There will never
be another Van Gogh.

Now think about this: Who painted Van Gogh? I'm serious. Who
created that great artist? I did. I'm what you might call the Meta-
Creator. That means I create things that create other things. That's
how creative I am. I am the original. I was the first being ever. Nothing
existed before Me. Everything that exists does so because of Me. So
how can you compare Me to objects or imaginary gods? Nothing
compares to Me.

The Original,
>God

== == ==    == == == == == == == == ==

# DESPERATE IS GOOD

**Blessed are the poor in spirit, for
theirs is the kingdom of heaven.**

Matthew        5:3

---------------------------------------------

My Wonderful Child,

>Have you ever come to the end of your rope? Have you ever prayed,
"God, please help me. I can't do it myself"? That's what it's like to be
poor in spirit. Being poor in spirit means that you desperately need
Me, and you know it. The truth is, everybody desperately needs Me.
But not everybody knows it.

If your car is almost out of gas and you know it, how is that a good
thing? Well, it's better than your car being almost out of gas and you
*not* knowing it. If you know you can't do it on your own, you are
blessed, because you'll have to pray, "God, help!" And people who
pray that prayer see My power at work, and circumstances change for
the better. Are you desperate for Me in your life? Then cry out and
prepare to experience My transforming power.

Your Mighty King,
>God

== == ==    == == == == == == == == ==

# WAS JESUS SURPRISED?

**But Jesus . . . knew mankind to the core.**

**John**        **2:24** TLB

-------------------------------------------

Dear Child,

>Jesus had every reason to be disillusioned by the people around Him. The Pharisees were jealous of His popularity; the Romans were suspicious of His power. In His hometown, people gave Him no respect. On the road, some people followed Him just because they thought His miracles were cool. Even His best friends let Him down. They swore they'd never betray Him, but when push came to shove, they all bailed, and Jesus was alone.

Was He surprised? Not in the least. He understood human nature for two reasons. To begin with, He was a human being and part of the human family. He still is. The other reason is that He was with Me when I created human beings. Your weakness never surprises Him. He knows you as you are, and He loves you anyway. So do I.

Your Loving Father,
>God

== == ==  == == == == == == == == ==

# ANY TIME IS A GOOD TIME

**You, Lord, have never forsaken those who seek you.**

**Psalm          9:10**

-----------------------------------------------

My Dear Child,

>Have you ever wanted to join a group, only to get rejected? Imagine that you tried out for a play. You practiced every night for the audition. When the audition came, you did your best and poured your heart out. Then the director told you, "Sorry, you're no good. Next." That would hurt. It might make you never want to try out for a play again.

I will never reject you. I'm not like that director. I think you are wonderful. I want to talk to you anytime. I want you to be part of what I'm doing. I always have time to listen to you and be with you. I want to hear about your day. I want to hear your hopes and dreams. Any time you want to be with Me, I will make time for you. So don't be afraid. I will never reject you.

Your Loving Father,
>God

== == ==    == == == == == == == == ==

# DO YOU KNOW YOUR JOB?

**John [the Baptist] replied, "God in heaven appoints each man's work. My work is to prepare the way for that man [Jesus] so that everyone will go to him."**

John          3:27-28 TLB

---------------------------------------------

Dear Child,

>John the Baptist was Jesus' cousin. He dressed in animal skins and ate a weird health-food diet. John was unusual, but people were attracted to listen to him anyway. John was one of a few people who actually knew that Jesus was the Messiah, and he understood how I wanted him to use that knowledge. I used John's gift of honest speech to call people away from their sins and toward their Savior. John's followers tried to make him jealous of Jesus, but he wouldn't go there. He knew that his job was not to be the Savior, but to help others *know* the Savior.

Would it surprise you to know that everybody was created to use their unique gifts to do the same job that John did—to point others to Jesus? Even you! Let Me show you how.

Your Loving Boss,
>God

== == ==     == == == == == == == == ==

# GET REAL

Jesus replied, ". . . it's not where we worship that counts,
but how we worship—is our worship spiritual and real?
Do we have the Holy Spirit's help? For God is Spirit,
and we must have his help to worship as we should."

John 4:     21,23-24 TLB

-------------------------------------------

Dear Child,

>There are so many different kinds of churches—from huge, ornate city
churches with elaborate stained-glass windows, to small, simple
churches built of wood on country roads. There are churches that meet
in tents and some that meet in homes like people did in Bible times.

If you asked Me to decide which kind of church I like best, I'd have to
tell you that it's not the building that makes the church, it's the people.
Where they worship doesn't matter one bit to Me. It's how they
worship that's important. Are they focused on My truth? Are they filled
with My Spirit? Are they humble and grateful and loving? These are
the questions that truly matter. Be real when you worship. Bring your
honest heart to Me.

The One You Worship,
>God

== == ==    == == == == == == == == ==

# DON'T WAIT TO PRAISE ME

**Can those in the grave declare your lovingkindness?
Can they proclaim your faithfulness?**

**Psalm**　　　**88:11** TLB

---------------------------------------------

Dear Child,

>Nobody wants to talk about death, but everybody dies. If you want a steady job, become an undertaker. You'll always have plenty of work. People die. That's a fact of life on earth. Once you're dead, you can't tell your friends about Me. Once they are dead, they can't choose Me. When you die, the time for choosing is over.

With that in mind, praise Me while others can still hear you. Sure, you'll praise Me in Heaven, but who on earth will be able to hear you then? Love people while you can. Be kind to people while you can. Tell people about Me and My love while you can. Believe Me, they'll be glad you didn't wait until later.

Your Salvation,
>God

== == ==　　== == == == == == == == ==

# TRY FEASTING ON MY WILL

Meanwhile, the disciples were urging Jesus to eat. "No,"
he said, "I have some food you don't know about. . . .
My nourishment comes from doing the will of God
who sent me, and from finishing his work."

**John 4:    31–32,34 TLB**

-------------------------------------------

Dear Child,

>It's easy to get so focused on physical things that you miss the
spiritual. Spiritual things are easy to miss because they are invisible,
but they matter big time. Why? I'm a spiritual being, and so are you.
Your spirit is the most important part of who you are.

Because the disciples were mostly fishermen who were used to their
physical world of nets and boats and fish, many times they missed
Jesus' spiritual lessons. Once when they urged Him to eat His supper,
He confused them by telling them that His food was to do My will and
finish My work.

Have you ever tasted that kind of food? Nothing in this world will
satisfy your spiritual hunger like doing My will. Try it, you'll like it!

The One Who Feeds You,
>God

== == ==    == == == == == == == == ==

# JESUS WAS REAL

**Because he himself suffered when he was tempted,
he is able to help those who are being tempted.**

**Hebrews          2:18**

-------------------------------------------

Dear Child,

>Some people think of Jesus as a marble statue with no blood running through His veins, or as a man so removed from reality that He never got to climb out of His stained-glass window and into real life. Not true.

Jesus was a flesh-and-blood human being as real as you are. He got hungry and tired; He laughed with His friends and cried when He was sad. He was a teenager just like you. And this one might surprise you: He was even tempted to do the wrong things. Resisting temptation was hard for Him, too, the same way it's hard for you.

But the good news is this: You don't have to try to hide your temptations from Jesus, because He understands. And when you need strength to stand against your temptations, you can go to Him. He can help you, and He will.

Your Father and His,
>God

== == ==    == == == == == == == == ==

# DO YOU WANT TO GET WELL?

**When Jesus saw him and knew how long he had been ill, he asked him, "Would you like to get well?"**

**John          5:6 TLB**

------------------------------------------

Dear Child,

>Once Jesus met a man who had been sick for thirty-eight years. He asked that man a surprising question: "Do you want to get well?" Seems like a no-brainer, doesn't it—like anyone would want to stay sick? But the truth is, some people hold on to their sickness. Maybe they're used to being sick and don't want to change. Maybe they use their sickness to control other people. Maybe they like the attention they get from being sick.

If you are sick—if you have chronic headaches, an eating disorder, an addiction, or whatever—ask yourself, "Do I really want to get well?" I hope you answered yes. If so, pray for My healing power.

Your Healer,
>God

== == ==     == == == == == == == == ==

# CLOSER THAN A PHONE CALL

**We do not know what to do, but our eyes are upon you.**

**2 Chronicles       20:12**

-------------------------------------------

Dear Child,

>I know how confusing your life can seem at times. When you don't know what to do, wouldn't it be nice to have a little video game called Easy Answers? Just flip it on, and it tells you what you need to know. Or maybe you'd like somebody wise and experienced sitting by the phone twenty-four hours a day with the right advice for each situation.

Life on this planet is not that simple. It's tough at times. But My book, the Bible, is full of answers. Read it. You'll see. And My Son, Jesus, has walked ahead of you through the obstacle course called life. Keep your eyes on Him when you don't know what to do. Talk to Him every time you're confused. You'll find out He's even closer than your telephone. So am I.

Your Father,
>God

== == ==    == == == == == == == == ==

# WE MAKE A GREAT TEAM!

**Do not fear, for I am with you; do not be dismayed, for I am your God. I will strengthen you and help you; I will uphold you with my righteous right hand.**

Isaiah          41:10

---------------------------------------------

My Child,

>In sports, it's fun to be on a good team. That way, when you go out against a tough opponent, the strong players on your side increase your chances of winning. Trusting your life to Me puts you on the most powerful team in the universe. You are lining up at the 50-yard line alongside Me, My Son, and My Holy Spirit, not to mention an enormous host of angels and all the saints who have gone before you! Trust Me, you're on the winning side! I'm not bragging—that's just the way it is.

So here's My advice to you today. Don't be afraid and never give up, no matter how bad things look. I am your God. I'm here to help you. I'm here to hold you up when you feel like throwing in the towel and quitting. Go on—get in the game. And when things get tough, remember that I'm on your side!

The Ultimate Athlete,
>God

== == ==    == == == == == == == == ==

# YOU CAN'T EVEN IMAGINE

**No eye has seen, no ear has heard, no mind has conceived
what God has prepared for those who love him.**

1 Corinthians          2:9

-------------------------------------------

My Dear Child,

>Have you ever gone to a really fun camp? For an entire week, you
went from the ropes course to horseback riding to hiking to swimming
to fun games and plays. The fun never stopped. But the fun at that
camp wasn't accidental. All sorts of people were preparing all year
long to make sure that all those activities would be ready for you
when you showed up.

In the same way, I've been preparing Heaven for you. I've had a lot of
time to work on it. I made the earth in six days, and it's pretty
amazing. I've been preparing Heaven for thousands of years. You
can't even imagine how awesome it's going to be. But even before
you get here, I have prepared a wonderful life for you to live on earth.
So love Me. Follow Me. I've got great things prepared for you.

Your Heavenly Host,
>God

== == ==    == == == == == == == == ==

# DON'T LET THE ROCKS STEAL YOUR THUNDER

**"God has given us a King!" they exulted. . . . But some**
**of the Pharisees among the crowd said, "Sir, rebuke your**
**followers for saying things like that!" [Jesus] replied, "If they**
**keep quiet, the stones along the road will burst into cheers!"**

Luke        19:38-40 TLB

---

Dear Child,

>Would it surprise you to know that praise for My Son is actually programmed into creation? One way or another, praise is going to erupt from this planet—praise for His goodness, mercy, and power. It can't be shut up or held back or snuffed out. If you stop it in one place, it'll burst out somewhere else.

One day, when a crowd was cheering for Jesus and singing His praises, some jealous Pharisees told Jesus to make them stop. Jesus just smiled and said, "If these people keep quiet, the praise will come from somewhere, even if the stones along the road have to cheer!"

You were born to celebrate Him. So don't miss the concert! Don't let a stack of rocks steal your thunder!

The Lord Who Loves Worship,
>God

== == ==    == == == == == == == == ==

# YOU'RE NO DOG!

**Do not love sleep or you will grow poor;
stay awake and you will have food to spare.**

**Proverbs          20:13**

--------------------------------------------

My Child,

>How do you feel about work? Do you hate it? Well, you better get used to it, because work will be a part of your life. Everybody works. What about a housewife? Of course she works. What about retired people? They get to work at what they want, but most retired people still work at something.

If all you want to do is lounge around all day, you should have been born a dog. But I didn't make you a dog. I made you a person. People work. Even in the garden, Adam and Eve worked. Work isn't a bad thing. It's something I intend for you to do, and you can enjoy it. Do the work I've given you to do. Even if you don't like it, decide to do it anyway. Later, I'll reward you for your faithfulness and give you more exciting work to do.

Your Boss,
>God

== == ==    == == == == == == == == ==

# YOU HAVE ME CONFUSED WITH SOMEONE ELSE

**I did not come to judge the world, but to save it.**

**John          12:47**

---------------------------------------------

Precious Child,

>Do you feel like Jesus is out to get you for every mistake you make?
You've got it all wrong. Jesus doesn't want to judge you or anybody. If
Jesus wanted to judge the world, He would have come on a big horse
and cut down all His enemies. Instead, Jesus came as a sacrifice, to
die in your place and save you from evil.

Yes, Jesus will come back on a big horse to judge the world. But until
then, that's not what He's about. Jesus is in the business of helping
people—rescuing them, giving them a way out, cutting them slack,
and showing them a better way. Jesus loves you. He's not mad at
you. He wants to help you. I feel the same way about you. Too many
people think of Me as some angry guy throwing lightning bolts. That's
not Me; that's Zeus. I only want to help you.

Your Savior,
>God

== == ==    == == == == == == == == ==

# NOTHING IS IMPOSSIBLE

**Jesus replied, "What is impossible
with men is possible with God."**

Luke          18:27

-------------------------------------------

Dear Child,

>What kind of person are you? Are you an impossibility person or a possibility person? An impossibility person looks at tough challenges and sees all the reasons they can't be done—all the impossibilities, so to speak. A possibility person looks at those same challenges and sees the possibilities.

The possibility person says, "Sure, it may be impossible if all you've got going for you is your own human strength and resources. But that's not all I've got going for me. I've got God and His strength and resources. All of Heaven is on My side, and everything is possible!" So no matter what your challenge is today, remember that I'm in it with you because I love you. And nothing—absolutely nothing—is impossible with Me.

The Lord of Possibilities,
>God

== == ==    == == == == == == == == ==

# TURN AROUND AND SEE ME HERE

**I am the LORD; that is my name! I will not give my glory to another or my praise to idols.**

Isaiah                    42:8

---------------------------------------------

Dear Child,

>If you could catch a glimpse of how much I love you, it would change you. If you could see the consuming fire of My love, it would shock you. You'd turn around and look at Me and there would be no words to express your amazement. I am the Lord—that's who I am. I long for a relationship with you that is more real, more honest, and more powerful than any other relationship in your life. I have so much to share with you. I don't want you to get so tangled up in the cheap stuff that you're blind to Me.

Think about it. Is there anything you've made a little god out of? Is there something so important to you that it's coming between us? Don't let anything else take center place in your heart. Turn around and see Me here.

I Am the Lord,
>God

== == ==    == == == == == == == == ==

# SPEAK MY TRUTH

The nations rage, the kingdoms totter; he utters
his voice, the earth melts. The Lord of hosts is
with us; the God of Jacob is our refuge.

Psalm        46:6-7 RSV

-------------------------------------------

Dear Child,

>Do you ever watch the news? If you do, you know what an uproar
the world is in most of the time. There are wars scattered all across
the globe. People are killing each other for every kind of reason, most
of them motivated by greed and a hunger for power. Families are
being uprooted and separated. Innocent children are suffering. How I
long to be a refuge to those people who will cry out to Me! But lots of
them don't even know I exist.

I need you to help bring My truth into this world at war. I need you to
speak with My voice so that people will know how close I am and how
much I care. In the middle of every kind of conflict, I am waiting for a
chance to shelter My people.

The Lord of Hosts,
>God

== == ==    == == == == == == == == ==

# STAY UNDER THE WATERFALL

**Keep yourselves in God's love as you wait for the mercy of our Lord Jesus Christ to bring you to eternal life.**

**Jude**      **21**

-------------------------------------------

Dear Child,

>If you are a Christian, if you have asked Jesus to be in control of your life, then you are going to Heaven. That's great, but how are you supposed to live until then? Well, from now until the day you die, the most important thing you can do is stay in My love.

My love is like a waterfall. It's always pouring down over you from Heaven. My love will clean you, refresh you, restore you, and feed you. Make sure you stay under the waterfall of My love. That means reading the Bible. It means setting apart some time every day just to listen to Me. It means talking to Me when things are going bad and when things are going good. To stay in My love means to obey Me. Eventually, you'll be here in Heaven with Me. Until then, stay in My love.

Your Constant Love-Giver,
>God

== == ==　== == == == == == == == ==

# I'VE GOT A PLAN

**Many are the plans in a man's heart, but it is the Lord's purpose that prevails.**

**Proverbs          19:21**

-------------------------------------------

Dear Child,

>So many people get their spiritual lives turned around backwards. With good intentions, they wake up every morning thinking, *Now, what can I do for God today?* They use their creative energy to hatch what they consider great plans for My kingdom. Then they roll up their sleeves and start working feverishly to accomplish their own plans. But they never ask Me what I want. That's like your parents buying you an expensive birthday present without once considering what you had in mind.

You see, I have plans of My own I want to involve you in. So learn to listen for My voice. Look around. Find out where I'm already at work and join Me there. You will discover the excitement of working with Me to bring My plans to completion.

The Ultimate Planner,
>God

== == ==    == == == == == == == == ==

# I'LL HELP YOU GET UNSTUCK

Come quickly, Lord, and answer me, for my
depression deepens; don't turn away from me. . . .
Show me where to walk, for my prayer is sincere.

Psalm          143:7-8 TLB

-------------------------------------------

Dear Child,

>Do you know how it feels to be depressed? It's a little bit like you're
paralyzed and can't put one foot in front of the other. Even getting out
of the bed feels like trying to climb out of quicksand. Making the
smallest decision takes too much energy. You feel like you're caught
in a revolving door—unable to stop turning. Worst of all, you can't
remember how to feel normal and happy.

If you ever feel depressed, talk to Me. Get real with Me. I want to
help. I'll show you how to exit from that revolving door of indecision.
I'll show you where to walk, one small step at a time. Trust Me. I have
great plans for your future. Good days are ahead.

Your Map to Better Times,
>God

== == ==    == == == == == == == == ==

# WANT A BLESSING?

**Honor your father and mother,
that you may have a long, good life.**

Exodus     20:12 TLB

------------------------------------------

Dear Child,

>Some kids make their parents' lives miserable by refusing to cooperate with anything they ask. Some kids pretend to cooperate but do what they want instead. Some even tell off their parents to their faces. I'm asking you to honor your parents. Stick up for them. Get along with them. Show them love, even if they aren't the kind of parents you would like them to be. Cooperate! (If you are being physically abused, that would be an exception. Tell someone—a pastor or school counselor—who can help you.)

I have put your parents in charge of you and your family, and your good treatment of them will bring a blessing to you. You'll learn to respect yourself and others by respecting your parents. You'll live a long, good life, and this is what I want for you.

Your Heavenly Parent,
>God

== == ==    == == == == == == == == ==

# TELL IT LIKE IT IS

**Better is open rebuke than hidden love.**

Proverbs        27:5

---------------------------------------------

Dear Child,

>Who is your friend—the person who tells you, "Hey, you've got a big piece of spinach in your teeth," or the person who says, "You look just fine"? Well, if you do have spinach in your teeth, then the person who told you about it is your friend. Conflict is not necessarily bad. If one of your friends has a problem, tell them.

Don't do it in a mean way. Do it because you love them and want to help them. Do your friends smoke or drink or do drugs? Be honest. Tell them how much it bothers you to see them destroying their health. If you are the one doing something harmful, I hope you have a friend who's honest enough with you to confront you about it. Sometimes friends have to get real with each other, even when it's uncomfortable. Not everything is always smiles and laughs. That's okay. A real friend is not afraid to speak the truth.

Your Friend,
>God

== == ==    == == == == == == == == ==

# A REFLECTION OF YOURSELF

**As in water face reflects face,
so the heart of man reflects man.**

**Proverbs        27:19 NASB**

-------------------------------------------

Dear Child,

>Looking into the face of another person is like looking into a mirror and seeing your own reflection. You're seeing the potential for good or evil that is in every person. What you choose to do with your potential will determine who you become. When you hate the bad qualities you see in someone else, remember that the potential for those qualities is in you, too. When you admire the good qualities you see in someone else, remember that the potential for those same qualities is also in you.

Let Me help you develop all the good things that are possible in you, so you can become all you were created to be. Most of all, look into the face of My Son, and let Me make you more like Him.

Your Father,
>God

== == ==    == == == == == == == == ==

# WHY DID YOU DO IT?

**Love does no harm to its neighbor.**

**Romans        13:10**

-------------------------------------------

Dear Child,

>If I cut you with a knife, do I love you? That depends. If I'm a thief trying to steal your money, of course I don't love you. But if I'm a doctor performing surgery on you to save your life, then yes, I do love you. It doesn't just matter what you do to someone, it also matters why you do it.

Have you ever told on someone who was breaking the rules? Why did you do it? If you did it just so you could see that person get in trouble, you did not act out of love. But if you did it because you knew that person was in danger of ruining his life by breaking the rules, you did it out of love. When telling on someone will make things better in the long run, that's when it's the loving thing to do. Love doesn't always look like love. But if you are truly helping someone, your actions are motivated by love.

Your Helper,
>God

== == ==    == == == == == == == == ==

# HEART-TO-HEART TALK

**Your Father knows what you need before you ask Him.**

**Matthew**     **6:8** NASB

--------------------------------------------

Dear Child,

>How would you describe prayer? Is it just telling Me what you need? Would it surprise you to hear Me say that I already know what you need? After all, I made you. I thought you up and put you together.

If there is something missing in your life right now, I know what it is before you even ask Me. In fact, I know before you know. For instance, you may feel uneasy and restless. You think you're just bored. But I may look inside your heart and see that the uneasiness is really a guilty feeling—that you need to apologize to someone but you don't want to face up to it.

Instead of always telling Me what you need, why don't you ask Me to show you exactly what it is? Prayer is the two of us talking it over. Let's have a heart-to-heart talk.

Your Father,
>God

== == ==    == == == == == == == == ==

# UP CLOSE AND PERSONAL

**The Word became flesh, and dwelt among us, and we saw His glory, glory as of the only begotten from the Father, full of grace and truth.**

**John          1:14 NASB**

---------------------------------------------

Dear Child,

>Jesus was truth in human form. He was My Word walking around in human skin. He had eyes and teeth and a smile and fingerprints and toenails and everything that makes up a regular person. I wrapped up all of My wisdom, My ideas, and even My personality in His human package.

"Now Son," I said to Jesus, "I want You to go to earth and live alongside My people. They need Me, but most of them are not finding Me. So go and show them what My love is like, up close and personal." Don't wonder what I'm like. Trust Me. When you look at the life of Jesus, you're really seeing Me.

The Father of Jesus,
>God

== == ==    == == == == == == == == ==

# SHOW ME LOVE

**The only thing that counts is faith expressing itself through love.**

Galatians          5:6

---------------------------------------------

My Wonderful Child,

>If you believe in Me, don't just say, "I believe in God." If you believe in Me, love people like I do. Once a bunch of students built a go-cart for a science project. Their teacher said, "Kids, I believe your cart is going to work." But when the students asked him if he wanted to take a ride in it, the teacher quickly said, "No way!" When it came to putting his life on the line, that teacher didn't really believe in his students, regardless of what he said.

I want you to put your life on the line for Me. If it means defending someone who's getting picked on, do it. If you lose some friends by loving the outcasts, that proves you care more about Me than about being popular. If you really believe in Me, you won't just say so, you'll act like it.

Your Father,
>God

== == ==    == == == == == == == == ==

# THIS IS NO TIME TO QUIT

**Why are you in despair, O my soul? And why have you become disturbed within me? Hope in God, for I shall yet praise Him, the help of my countenance and my God.**

**Psalm          42:11** NASB

--------------------------------------------

Dear Child,

>Lots of things can rain on your parade. Feeling like a failure can. Unkind words can sting your ego, stomp on your emotions, and make you want to hide inside yourself so no one can ever hurt you again.

On days like that, instead of hiding, here's what I want you to do. Remember that self-pity never solved a thing. So stand up tall, lift up your head, and listen. You are valuable—priceless in fact! You are a child of the Most High God. All the power of Heaven is on your side today. This is no time to quit. I want you to speak to your own soul like David did. Say, "Soul, get up! It's time to stop moping and start praising! It's time to get in gear and get back in the game."

The One Who Treasures You,
>God

== == ==    == == == == == == == == ==

# STOP THE WAR!

**Christ himself is our way of peace.**

**Ephesians**     2:14 TLB

------------------------------------------

Dear Child,

>Judging by the amount of violence reported on the news, you can tell that real peace is hard to find. Wars and bloodshed are everywhere on every continent. But there is an invisible war going on right now in your own life. The fighting takes place inside your heart. Instead of accepting My acceptance, you are constantly condemning yourself. Instead of receiving My grace, you are constantly beating yourself up for not being good enough.

Won't you let Me give you peace? Won't you let My Spirit end the battle? Won't you rest in the awareness that I am in the process of remaking you into the likeness of My Son? Stay close to Me, trust Me to work in your life, and you'll find inner serenity.

The Lord of Peace,
>God

== == ==   == == == == == == == == ==

# FLY IT HIGH!

**He has taken me to the banquet hall,
and his banner over me is love.**

**Song of          Solomon 2:4**

-------------------------------------------

My Dear Child,

>During the Middle Ages when an army went to war, the king's banner would be flown overhead. The banner told all who saw it, "This army belongs to that king." There is a banner for My kingdom, too. My banner over you is love. People will know you belong to Me because of My love for you.

I want to bless you. I want to make a big deal over you. I want to have a party for you. Don't be shy. Let Me love you. The more you let Me love you, the more people will see that you belong to Me, and they will want a relationship with Me. If you don't let Me love you, if you always mope around wondering whether I love you, who is going to want to know Me? Receive My love. Celebrate Me. I celebrate you every day. I love you so much. You are awesome!

The Lover of Your Soul,
>God

== == ==    == == == == == == == == ==

# A KEY TO HAPPINESS

**Give thanks to him and praise his name.
For the Lord is good and his love endures forever.**

**Psalm        100:4-5**

---------------------------------------------

Dear Child,

>Did you ever wish you had a key to happiness? Guess what? There is one. You might shake your head and say, "No way. This'll never work." But trust Me. My children have been turning this key for a couple of thousand years, and it really does lead to happiness. Ready?

Always thank Me in everything. That's right . . . always . . . in everything. I can just hear you saying, "Surely, He doesn't expect Me to thank Him for the bad stuff." No, I didn't say *for* everything; I said *in* everything. I am a good Father. I am busy working every single thing out for your good—even the bad stuff. The devil is the one causing all the bad stuff. But if you will praise Me in the midst of even the bad things that come your way, it will be the key to unlock My blessing. I can turn even the bad things around for your good. So turn the key and give Me praise.

The Lord of the Key,
>God

== == ==    == == == == == == == == ==

# TRUST ME, YOU'RE NOT A LOSER!

**Create in me a clean heart, O God, and
renew a steadfast spirit within me.**

**Psalm        51: 10** NASB

-------------------------------------------

Dear Child,

>I'm going to ask you a tough question. Are you down on yourself
about something? Maybe you despise the way you look. Maybe you
made some dumb remark or acted like a moron, and you keep
replaying it in your head. Listen, I love your looks, and I'm proud of
your mind. Trust Me, you're no loser!

But there is something I do want to change about you. I want to
change your heart and your spirit. I want to give you a heart so clean
and a spirit so new that you'll be able to love yourself as I love you.
You won't constantly be on your own case. When you've done
something wrong, you'll confess it and accept My forgiveness and live
without this constant self-condemnation.

The One Who Cleans Hearts,
>God

== == ==    == == == == == == == == ==

# IT WAS FOR YOU

**It is a trustworthy statement, deserving full acceptance,
that Christ Jesus came into the world to save sinners.**

**1 Timothy       1:15 NASB**

---------------------------------------------

Dear Child,

>Why did My Son show up on planet earth? Why did He lead the life
of a normal Jewish boy—raised by simple parents in a shabby town,
taught a trade, trained in a synagogue school? Why did He travel
dusty roads speaking to fishermen and tax collectors, farmers and
housewives? Why did He silently tolerate a humiliating arrest and a
mock trial for something He didn't do? Why did He suffer a painful
death on a cross that was reserved for criminals?

It was for sinners. Who are the sinners? Everyone who has ever
failed at all. Everyone who has been unable to live a perfect life. In
short, everyone. It was for you He lived and died and rose again so
that you would have a way to live as My child. My free gift of salvation
is available for the taking. Will you receive Him now?

Your Father,
>God

== == ==    == == == == == == == == ==

# THE TRUTH

**Long ago, even before he made the world, God chose us to be his very own. . . . His unchanging plan has always been to adopt us into his own family by sending Jesus Christ to die for us.**

**Ephesians       1:4-5 TLB**

---------------------------------------------

Dear Child,

>At a press conference once, a famous Christian scholar named Karl Barth was asked, "What is the most profound truth you've ever learned in all your studies?" Dr. Barth's answer was surprisingly simple: "Jesus loves me, this I know, for the Bible tells me so."

You may be in college or high school or even younger, but it doesn't matter how many years you devote to your studies on any topic, you will never discover a more life-changing truth than the truth of My Son's love for you. When you feel bogged down in schoolwork, stressed out by your friendships, or critical of yourself, steady your life in that rock-solid reality. Jesus loves you. My plan has always been to adopt you into My family through His awesome love.

Your Father,
>God

== == ==    == == == == == == == == ==

# TAKE ME AT MY WORD

**Heal me, O LORD, and I will be healed; save me
and I will be saved, for You are my praise.**


Jeremiah     17:14 NASB


---------------------------------------------

Dear Child,

>When you begin to take Me at My word, so many things will change
in your life. I have said that you are My own creation, and yet at
times, you see yourself as less than worthwhile. I have said that I
have a plan and a purpose for your life, and yet there are days when
you feel hopeless. I have said that I love you and will never leave
you, and yet at times, you feel unloved and alone. I have told you not
to be afraid, and yet you battle so many fears.

My words contain power, but they cannot help you until you believe
them. I am a guide, a friend, and a Father, but I cannot touch you
unless you let Me near. The way to life is simple and straightforward.
Know Me, trust My Word completely, call on Me, and I'll take action in
your life.

The Healer,
>God

== == ==    == == == == == == == == ==

# BREAD FOR THE HUNGRY HEART

**Man shall not live by bread alone, but by every word that proceeds from the mouth of God.**

Matthew          4:4 RSV

-------------------------------------------

Dear Child,

>You could eat biscuits for breakfast, sandwiches for lunch, and pizza for dinner and still have a hollow heart. Bread can fill a hungry stomach, but only My Word can nourish a hungry heart. Only My Word can fill up your inner hunger for the truth.

What is the truth? The truth is, I love you. The truth is, I created you to live in a relationship with Me. The truth is, when your sin separated you from Me, I sent Jesus to build a bridge to My mercy. That bridge was a cross. Only these truths can fill you and fuel you for the difficult journey ahead. So eat bread for your physical hunger, but feed on My Word when your heart is hungry for the truth.

The Living Bread,
>God

== == ==    == == == == == == == == ==

# COME THIRSTY

Those who believe him discover that God is a fountain
of truth. For this one—sent by God—speaks God's words,
for God's Spirit is upon him without measure or limit.

John        3:33-34 TLB

---------------------------------------------

Dear Child,

>People who come looking for Jesus find Him. Thirsty people who are willing to believe discover a fountain of truth. When Jesus lived on earth, that's how it was. People who were open to His words drank the living water. But people who plugged their ears with doubts usually went away thirsty.

It's the same today. When you look for Jesus in My book, the Bible, you always have a choice. You can read with openness and trust and find everything you've been thirsting for, or you can be too cool for the simple truth, determined to find all the contradictions and loopholes. If so, you'll close the book and go away thirsty and unfulfilled. The choice is yours. Trust Me, and I'll quench your thirst. That's a promise.

The Fountain of Truth,
>God

== == ==    == == == == == == == == ==

# LOVE THEM ALL

**Give to the one who asks you, and do not turn away from the one who wants to borrow from you.**

Matthew        5:42

-------------------------------------------

Dear Child,

>Street people are an interesting bunch. Many are dirty, some are lazy, some are liars, some are dangerous, some are crazy, but many are just out of work. None of that matters to Me. I love them all, and I want you to love them, too. Just be wise about it.

I don't want you to give some guy money so he can go buy alcohol. If someone says they need money for food, why not offer to pay for their meal at a nearby fast-food restaurant? If they're just scamming for money, they'll say no, and you're off the hook. If they're really hungry, they'll say yes, and you'll get to share a meal and My Good News with someone I love. I care about poor people, and I want you to care, too. If you don't care, who will?

The Bread of Life,
>God

== == ==    == == == == == == == == ==

# THE LOVE SUIT

**Do everything in love.**

**1 Corinthians     16:14**

--------------------------------------------

My Child,

>What if you had to wear a clown suit all day long? When you brushed your teeth in the morning, you looked in the mirror and saw a clown. When you walked down the street, your clown feet slapped the pavement. When you went to school, you were literally the class clown! How would it feel to do everything all day long as a clown?

Well, I want you to do everything in love. Walk down the street in love. When someone gets on your nerves, respond in love. When you go shopping in the mall, shop in love. What if everything you did all day long was done in love? If you wear a clown costume all day long, you're going to make a lot of people laugh. If you wear a love suit all day long, you're going to make a lot of people feel loved. And you won't even have to wear those floppy shoes.

Your Joy Giver,
>God

== == ==   == == == == == == == == ==

# A HERO WAITING TO HAPPEN

**The LORD is with you, O valiant warrior.**

**Judges        6:12** NASB

-------------------------------------------

Dear Child,

>When you feel like a flop or a failure, a weakling or a wimp, see yourself as I see you. In My eyes, you have the makings of a hero!

When the world looks for a hero, they look for a superman who's able to "leap tall buildings in a single bound." But I look for spiritual muscles, and that's where I see your potential. You can be a "spiritual warrior"— just like Gideon who conquered a huge army of Midianites with just three hundred men—just like Joshua who brought down the walls of Jericho because he trusted Me and followed My directions. Those are not just stories to entertain you. They are true stories I put in My Bible to build your faith. Believe Me. You're a hero waiting to happen!

Your General,
>God

== == ==    == == == == == == == == ==

# A MAN WITH A MISSION

**The Son of Man did not come to be served, but
to serve, and to give His life a ransom for many.**

**Mark          10:45** NASB

-------------------------------------------

Dear Child,

>If anybody had a right to live in a castle with lots of servants bowing
down to Him, it was Jesus. He was the ultimate King, and yet He
lived a simple life. He had a totally humble heart and a radically loving
Spirit. He didn't come to earth expecting everyone to make a big deal
about who He was. In fact, He didn't even let many people in on His
true identity. He dressed in the simplest clothes. He slept on the
ground. He made friends with real down-and-outers—lawbreakers,
tax collectors, and lepers.

Jesus was a man with a mission. He didn't come to be served but to
serve. He didn't come to take, but to give His life away as a ransom
for whomever would trust Him. Will you be one of those who does?

His Father and Yours,
>God

== == ==    == == == == == == == == ==

# GIUE ME A BREAK

**Observe the Sabbath day by keeping it holy, as the LORD your God has commanded you. Six days you shall labor and do all your work, but the seventh day is a Sabbath to the LORD your God. On it you shall not do any work.**

**Deuteronomy      5:12-14**

-------------------------------------------

Dear Child,

>You can't work all the time. Can a car race the entire Indy 500 without a pit stop? No. I made you the same way. You need a break. If I took a day off after making the world, and I'm God, then you can take a day off once a week, too.

You're thinking, *Right, my parents are really going to let me take a day off.* Here's how you do it—cut a deal with them where you agree to get all your work done before your day off. They'll be so amazed that you mowed the lawn a day early, they'll probably agree to it. On your day off, start by spending time with Me. Then do something different. Get outside. Go on a walk. Enjoy the world I made. Listen to Me, and I will tell you things on your day off that you weren't able to hear during your busy week. Try it and see. I'll meet you there.

The Lord of the Sabbath,
>God

== == ==    == == == == == == == == ==

# IT'S SIMPLE—REALLY

**Do for others what you want them to do for you.
This is the teaching of the laws of Moses in a nutshell.**

Matthew     7:12 TLB

-------------------------------------------

Dear Child,

>I bet you could make Me a list of all the things you want other people to do for you. You want your kid brother to leave your stuff alone. You want your mom and dad to listen when you're trying to talk to them. You want your teacher to give you a break on your algebra grade.

I'm asking you to start looking at your life from a totally different point of view. I'm asking you to start thinking about what those other people want and need instead of worrying so much about yourself and what you want. Try spending a little more time with your little brother—he might like that. Try listening to your parents when they talk to you. Try paying attention in algebra now and then. It's simple really. Think more about others than yourself.

The Lord of the Golden Rule,
>God

== == ==    == == == == == == == == ==

# GAME OUER

**What I mean, brothers, is that the time is short. . . .
For this world in its present form is passing away.**

1 Corinthians        7:29,31

-------------------------------------------

My Child,

>Believe it or not, the world is going to end. I'm not some crazy street preacher yelling, "The end is near." I'm God. And in My Bible I'm saying, "Time is short. The end is near." Were you thinking about messing around with sex or drinking or partying for a little while? Were you planning on getting serious about Me later? There's no time for that.

I've created you to do great things—things that are going to bless you and others—things that are going to make the world a better place. I'm waiting on you to get real with Me. I'm looking for anyone "crazy" enough to do it My way—not tomorrow, but now. Are you in or out? If you think your life doesn't matter, you're wrong. No one else can do what I have for you to do. This is not a game. It's real, and we're running out of time.

Your Motivator,
>God

== == ==    == == == == == == == == ==

# NO NERDS, JOCKS, OR SNOBS

**From now on we recognize no one
according to the flesh.**

**2 Corinthians     5:16** NASB

-------------------------------------------

Dear Child,

>Today I want you to do an experiment at school. I want you to
pretend that I'm giving you a pair of glasses with special lenses in
them. When you look at people through these glasses, you can see
people as I see them. That so-called nerd you think is embarrassing
is really brave and tenderhearted. That jock you think is stupid has a
heart capable of great wisdom. That cheerleader you think is so
snobby is really shy and insecure and needs a good friend.

Nothing is what it seemed to be before you put the glasses on. You
realize there are really no nerds, no jocks, and no snobs—only people,
My creations. And once you see them as I see them, I will help you
love them with My love. So put on My glasses and take a look!

The One with 20/20 Vision,
>God

== == ==    == == == == == == == == ==

# GOT A WHOLE LOT OF LOVE

**Your love, O L‍ord, reaches to the heavens,
your faithfulness to the skies.**

**Psalm          36:5**

---------------------------------------------

My Precious Child,

>My love is like no other love you know. Everybody has bad days.
People get sick of life, fed up, and just can't take it anymore. Has
anyone ever told you, "You're getting on my last nerve"? That person
is only human and just ran out of love.

But My love never runs out. I have more than enough. No matter how
bad you've been, and no matter how busy you think I am, I will never
be cruel. I'll never say a mean word to you. I'll never hurt you in any
way. I won't yell at you when you need Me to listen. I won't ignore you
when you need Me to pay attention. So don't be afraid to come to Me
anytime. I love you.

Your Best Friend,
>God

== == ==    == == == == == == == == ==

# SHARE EACH OTHER'S PROBLEMS

**Share each other's troubles and problems,
and so obey our Lord's command.**

Galatians        6:2 TLB

---------------------------------------------

Dear Child,

>Suppose your friend on the track team broke her leg and couldn't run for the rest of the season. Would you say to yourself, "Thank goodness it wasn't me!" or maybe, "Now that she's out of the running, I have a chance to place first in the mile"?

If those kinds of thoughts come into your mind, tell Me about them. I want you to represent Jesus in your friend's life. Try to imagine how she must feel. Offer some practical help, like carrying her books or giving her a ride to the track meets so she can still be part of the team from the sidelines. Sharing her problem is My plan for your life. Remember, Jesus could have stayed in Heaven and left you on earth without a friend, but instead He came. Now it's your turn.

The Lord of Compassion,
>God

== == ==    == == == == == == == == ==

# LOVE THE TRUTH

**Say just a simple "Yes, I will" or
"No, I won't." Your word is enough.**

Matthew          5:37 TLB

-------------------------------------------

Dear Child,

>Have you ever known anybody who seemed like they'd rather make
up a lie than tell the simple truth? Have you ever known anyone who
practiced exaggerating just to beef up whatever they were saying?
Have you ever known anyone who promised to be on time and
always arrived twenty minutes late? It's hard to trust people like that
or take them seriously.

I don't want you to live like that. Your integrity matters to Me. When
you tell the truth, it honors the other person, yourself, and Me. If you
aren't sure you can commit to something, don't promise you'll do it.
Say, "Let me pray (or think) about it, and I'll let you know." Let your
yes be yes and your no be no. Begin today to love the truth as much
as I do.

The One Who Is Truth,
>God

== == ==    == == == == == == == == ==

# GET EMOTIONAL

**Rejoice with those who rejoice;
mourn with those who mourn.**

**Romans 12:15** -------------------

------------------------

Dear Child,

>Have you ever proudly tried to share your excitement about a great report card with friends only to have them extinguish your joy with indifference? It hurts, doesn't it? So don't treat other people that same way. If a friend comes to you all excited about something, don't be jealous of her. Don't put down what she's done. If she's stoked about something, you be stoked about it, too.

Likewise, if one of your friends is feeling down, don't laugh at him. Don't tell him to just get over it. Feel what he feels. Care. Understand. Listen. My Son, Jesus, was full of compassion for everyone He met. That's what it's like to be part of the human family—you feel what other people feel. You get emotional. Forget being cool. Get real.

The Compassionate One,
>God

== == ==    == == == == == == == == ==

# LET'S SPEND SOME QUALITY TIME TOGETHER

**When he and his followers were alone,
Jesus explained everything to them.**

**Mark            4:34** NCV

---------------------------------------------

Dear Child,

>You are constantly on the move, surrounded by people and involved in activities. How can I get a word in edgewise? There is truth I want to show you, amazing things I want to share, but you'll never hear My voice unless you're willing to slow down and listen—to open the Bible and read.

For three years, the disciples spent part of each day alone with Jesus. He showed them My kingdom through teaching and example. In Him, they saw Me. And though there was a lot they didn't understand, later, the Holy Spirit helped them put the pieces together.

The mystery and miracle of His life is still here for you to discover, and His Spirit is still waiting to help you understand. So pull away from the noise. Be still and listen.

The One Who Speaks,
>God

== == ==    == == == == == == == == ==

# PUT YOUR FAITH IN ME

**Some trust in chariots and some in horses,
but we trust in the name of the LORD our God.**

**Psalm          20:7**

---------------------------------------

Dear Child,

>Remember reading about Moses leading My people out of Egypt?
They were almost to the Red Sea when Pharaoh and his army
decided to chase them down. So the army mounted powerful horses
and got into blazing chariots and came charging across the desert
after My people (most of whom were walking on foot). Did My people
really stand a chance against the whole powerful Egyptian army?

You bet they did! Why? They had put their trust in something stronger
than horses and chariots. They had a miracle-working God on their
side. I parted the Red Sea so My people could walk across, and
when the Egyptians showed up, I released all that water on top of
them—horses, chariots, and all. So when things seem hopeless, put
your faith in Me. I'm more powerful than any enemy!

Your Champion,
>God

== == ==    == == == == == == == == ==

# JUST PASSING THROUGH

**Since you call on a Father who judges each man's work impartially, live your lives as strangers here in reverent fear.**

**1 Peter          1:17**

-------------------------------------------

My Child,

>When you go to a weekend camp far away from your home, you can act differently. You can tell people things about yourself that you never would have told people at your school. You can risk more. Why? Because you might never see those other campers again.

Like that weekend camp, this planet is not your permanent home. Even if you live here for a hundred years, it's really not that long from My viewpoint. You're just passing through this life. When you die, if you've allowed Me to adopt you into My family, you'll spend the rest of eternity with Me in Heaven. So with that in mind, don't get too attached to this world. Don't worry about what people think about you. Just concern yourself with Me and My opinion. I am the One that matters, because I will be with you forever.

Your Eternal Father,
>God

== == ==    == == == == == == == == ==

# THINK ABOUT IT

**Within your temple, O God, we meditate on your unfailing love.**

**Psalm          48:9**

---------------------------------------------

Dear Child,

>When was the last time you meditated on My unfailing love? Meditating is just focusing on something and thinking about it for a while. When you spend time with Me, don't forget to listen. After you've talked to Me, after you've waited for Me to talk to you, after you've read the Bible, and after you've read this book, what comes next?

Do this for Me: Right now, just take five minutes to sit still and think about My love. I made everything. I can do anything. I made you. I love you so much that I sacrificed My Son so you and I could be together. I showed Myself to you. Just stop and think about that for a while.

Your Father,
>God

== == ==    == == == == == == == == ==

# REFERENCES

Unless otherwise indicated, all Scripture quotations are taken from the *Holy Bible, New International Version*® NIV®. Copyright © 1973, 1978, 1984 by International Bible Society. Used by permission of Zondervan Publishing House. All rights reserved.

Scripture quotations marked NASB are taken from the *New American Standard Bible.* Copyright © The Lockman Foundation 1960, 1962, 1963, 1968, 1971, 1972, 1973, 1975, 1977, 1995. Used by permission.

Verses marked THE MESSAGE are taken from *The Message,* copyright © by Eugene H. Peterson, 1993, 1994, 1995. Used by permission of NavPress Publishing Group.

Scripture quotations marked PHILLIPS are taken from the *New Testament in Modern English,* (Rev. Ed.) by J. B. Phillips. Copyright © 1958, 1960, 1972 by J.B. Phillips. Reprinted by permission of Macmillan Publishing Co., New York, New York.

Verses marked TLB are taken from *The Living Bible,* copyright ©1971. Used by permission of Tyndale House Publishers, Inc., Wheaton, Illinois 60189. All rights reserved.

Scripture quotations marked NCV are taken from *The Holy Bible, New Century Version,* copyright © 1987, 1988, 1991 by Word Publishing, Dallas, Texas 75039. Used by permission.

Scripture quotations marked KJV are taken from the *King James Version* of the Bible.

Scripture quotations marked RSV are taken from *The Revised Standard Version Bible,* copyright © 1952 by the Division of Christian Education of the Churches of Christ in the United States of America and is used by permission.

# ABOUT THE AUTHORS

**Claire Cloninger,** winner of five Dove awards for songwriting, also created the phenomenally successful musical *My Utmost for His Highest.* She has authored eleven books, including best-sellers *E-Mail from God for Teens, A Place Called Simplicity,* and *Dear Abba.* Claire and her husband, Robert, have two children and three grandchildren. They make their home in Baldwin County, Alabama.

**Curt Cloninger,** Claire's son, is the coauthor of *E-Mail from God for Teens.* Currently, he is employed as the Internet Administrator for Integrity Music and is the worship leader at the Mobile Vineyard Christian Fellowship. He spent two years in Youth With a Mission and has worked as a middle-school teacher, a high-school track coach, and a house parent in a children's home. He and his wife, Julie, are the parents of a daughter, Caroline.

If you have enjoyed this book, or if it has
impacted your life, we would like to hear from you.
Please contact us at:

Honor Books
Department E
P.O. Box 55388
Tulsa, Oklahoma 74155
Or by e-mail at info@honorbooks.com